Richard Webster was born in 1950. He studied English literature at the University of East Anglia where he has also taught. In 1985 he and his wife started The Orwell Bookshop in Southwold, Suffolk. His first book, *A Brief History of Blasphemy: Liberalism, Censorship and 'The Satanic Verses'*, was published in 1990. His intellectual biography of Freud, *Why Freud Was Wrong: Sin Science and Psychoanalysis*, was published by HarperCollins in 1995. His articles and reviews have appeared in the *Guardian*, the *New Statesman* and the *Times Literary Supplement*. He now lives in Oxford.

THE GREAT CHILDREN'S HOME PANIC

Richard Webster

Richard Webster died suddenly in June 2011. He would hope that those who read this book might be inspired in some small way to battle against injustice, vigorously and relentlessly, as he always did.

The Orwell Press

First published in Great Britain in 1998 by
The Orwell Press
10 Radley House
Marston Ferry Road
Oxford OX2 7EA

ISBN 0 9515922 2 X

Typeset by Avocet Typeset, Brill, Aylesbury, Bucks
Printed and bound by Cox & Wyman Ltd, Reading

Contents

The names of all witnesses and complainants in the cases which are discussed have been changed.

A Note to the Reader

THIS IS AN IMPROMPTU book. It was originally conceived in January 1998 as a pamphlet containing a single article. In the course of the next month it grew in size. Of the three articles which are now collected in it, the first appeared in the *Guardian* on 20 January 1997 – the day before the North Wales Tribunal held its first full public hearing. I am grateful to the *Guardian* for publishing a point of view which, at that time, had scarcely been expressed at all, and for allowing me to reproduce the article now.

The second article, 'Police, Care Workers and the Creation of False Allegations', was not originally intended for publication. It was written for private circulation among solicitors, barristers and others who had become involved with allegations of the kind I describe. A number of people have responded to this piece warmly and enthusiastically and they have urged me to make it more widely available.

The third article, 'The Great Children's Home Panic', was written especially for this book.

All these articles came to be written because, in the spring of 1996, I found myself almost by accident in the position of having to investigate a bizarre development in modern policing methods. The development in question was the entirely new kind of police operation employed to collect the thousands of retrospective allegations of abuse made against residential care workers over the past ten years. So numerous are the allegations which have been gathered in this way, and so horrifying is the picture which emerges from them, that many people have come to believe that 'children's homes' are synonymous with abuse and that, during a particular period in our recent history, it was the norm rather than the exception for residential workers to engage in the sexual abuse of those who were in their care.

This view of children's homes first began to emerge in about 1990 at almost exactly the same time that wild allegations about organised satanic abuse were beginning to be discredited. Over the next few years one particular idea gained currency among some social workers, child protection workers and journalists. This was the belief that children's homes had been infiltrated by organised groups of paedophiles. Many people remained sceptical, but within a small circle this view became accepted almost as an orthodoxy. During the spring and early summer of 1996 the idea was given much wider currency in the press and the media. So rarely was it challenged that by 1997, in an article in the *Guardian* which was not even about residential care, the respected feminist journalist Linda Grant could refer almost casually to children's homes being run by 'a bureaucracy of paedophiles'.

It was just such a belief – that children's homes might have been taken over by paedophile rings – that was held with great fervour by those who triggered the massive police inquiry into alleged abuse in North Wales which was launched in August 1991. It was the same belief which subsequently led to the investigation of the New Barns School in Toddington, Gloucestershire, and to the eventual destruction of this outstanding Quaker institution.

Similar concerns about paedophile rings were originally entertained by some of those who, in 1994, helped to launch an even larger investigation in Cheshire, just over the border from North Wales. Although it is not possible to give an exact figure for how many careworkers have now been arrested in Cheshire it seems clear that the figure is now well in excess of 100. In March 1998 the Cheshire Police confirmed that no fewer than twenty-five care workers had already been charged as a result of their investigations. Twenty-two of these careworkers have so far stood trial and the majority of these have been convicted and sentenced to long terms in prison.

North Wales and Cheshire are by no means the only areas where such massive police operations have been launched. Investigations are also in progress in Merseyside in South Wales, in north-east England and in a number of other regions. Even after this book was conceived news was released of another huge investigation into care homes in the Greater Manchester district. Slowly but surely our prisons are filling up with care workers who have been convicted as a result of the allegations which have been made during these investigations. How should we react to this extraordinary development?

It requires only a little knowledge of human nature to recognise that wherever adults and young people are placed together in residential settings – whether in boarding schools, in religious institutions or indeed in families – sexual abuse will sometimes take place. Care homes are no exception to this rule and some of those workers who are now in prison are there for no other reason than that they are guilty of the crimes of which they have been convicted. To this extent at least it may be said that the investigations in Cheshire, North Wales and elsewhere have served the purposes of justice.

But many of those who have direct knowledge of these investigations, including a significant number of solicitors and barristers, have become more and more disturbed by what appears to be happening. They are concerned above all about the manner in which allegations have been obtained and about the soundness of some of the convictions they have led to.

Whichever way we choose to interpret it, the large number of convictions now taking place is worrying. Have we suddenly woken up to a horrifying reality which we have only recently been able to acknowledge? Or have we unleashed a witch-hunt which is unable to discriminate between those who are guilty and those who are innocent and which, because of the huge power of individual police forces throughout the country, is already out of control?

To answer these questions in detail would take a full-length book, and there are many good reasons why such a book should be written. But as more and more care workers throughout the country find themselves under investigation because of allegations made during retrospective investigations, a more speedy response seems necessary. It is largely for this reason that I have published this impromptu collection of essays. I hope that it will throw some light on a phenomenon which journalists have frequently written about, but which few have taken the trouble to investigate in any depth.

Oxford, March 1998

Care Goes on Trial

(*Guardian*, 20 January 1997)

'THE RESIDENTIAL CARE system of this country is now on trial. These children's homes were supposed to provide care, but instead they dished out a diet of sadism by day and sodomy by night.' So said Labour Welsh affairs spokesman Rhodri Morgan in the House of Commons in June 1996. Tomorrow, as the North Wales Tribunal of Inquiry opens for its first full public session under the chairmanship of Sir Ronald Waterhouse, the trial Rhodri Morgan referred to will begin in earnest.

His words, though well-calculated to grab headlines in tabloid newspapers, can have done little to help establish the climate which is needed for a fair inquiry. The current tribunal, which is not expected to report until 1998, carries a very heavy burden of judicial responsibility. For it will be clear to any observer in Britain (or, for that matter, in Australia) that anxieties about paedophile rings operating in children's homes have by now spread beyond the boundaries of the former county of Clwyd.

Although Clwyd was one of the first counties in Britain to initiate a massive retrospective investigation into suspected abuse in care homes, an even bigger operation has since been mounted in neighbouring Cheshire. By the end of 1996 at least 100 care workers had been arrested in this one English county alone. Some twenty miles beyond Chester, Liverpool has become the centre of a third major investigation. If the North Wales Tribunal does not cast at least some light on the two neighbouring investigations – which, technically, lie beyond its terms of reference – many will regard the estimated £10 million that it is likely to cost as a colossal waste of public funds.

There can be no doubt at all that these investigations in the north-west have uncovered and brought to justice a small number of men who did indeed exploit the positions of trust which they held by abusing children in their care. But these inquiries have also led to a relatively large number of convictions whose soundness is, to say the least, open to question.

What is perhaps even more remarkable about these investigations is that, in one respect, their outcome has been entirely negative. For although they were launched with the aim of uncovering *organised* sexual abuse in care homes, no such evidence has ever been found. Speaking outside Chester Crown Court after the conviction of John Allen in 1995, Detective Superintendent Ackerley put it like this: 'We thought at first that there was a paedophile ring. Now we know that it was just two evil men.'

This highly significant negative finding is rarely reported. But it raises an interesting question. For once the paedophile-ring theory has been discarded for want of evidence it is difficult to explain why three police forces in a small corner of Britain have had to devote huge resources to an almost unprecedented kind of investigation. While it is possible that the roots of a massive conspiracy still lie undetected in North Wales, there is another yet more disturbing possibility, which has been obscured by careless talk about 'children's homes'. This term, with its implication that the allegations have themselves been made by children, is doubly misleading. For up to now the major investigations have focused almost exclusively not on children's homes, but on institutions which deal with exceptionally difficult adolescents, many of whom are young offenders.

Far from making their allegations as children, or even as teenagers, most of those who have made complaints of sexual abuse in the north-west have done so as adults. And the vast majority have made these claims not spontaneously, but in response to a police 'trawl' for evidence. Such trawls are intrinsically dangerous. In many cases police officers taking part in them are not only eager to receive allegations, but eager to believe them as well. Knowing nothing of the human qualities of the care workers who have been accused, and predisposed by the nature of their investigation to think the worst, they often find it extremely difficult to avoid demonising those under investigation and thus becoming emotionally committed to finding yet more allegations against them.

In some cases there is evidence that police officers have actively solicited allegations against individuals or that they have themselves held out the promise of compensation. And it is now common knowledge among former residents of care homes that allegations of sexual abuse can sometimes result in successful civil claims for amounts up to £100,000.

All in all, if a deliberate attempt were made to encourage false allegations, it would be difficult to better the conditions which result from the setting up of any large-scale retrospective inquiry. What has happened in North Wales, in Cheshire and in Liverpool, it would seem, is that large numbers of young men, many of whom belong to a culture in which financial gain traditionally goes hand in hand with some form of crime or dishonesty, have been presented with a hitherto undreamed-of opportunity. They have found themselves in a position where allegations against their former carers are being actively solicited by police officers and where any false allegation, provided it is made against an individual who attracts other allegations, is likely to be given massive professional and institutional support.

Of course some of the allegations which have been gathered in the north-west are genuine. And all such allegations should be investigated with the utmost seriousness. But in a disturbing number of cases internal or external evidence suggests that allegations have been fabricated. And all too often it would appear that false allegations have been believed not only by police officers, but also by the courts.

If this is so we must face up to the possibility that what has happened in the north-west is something which has happened on too many occasions before in American and European history: that, as a direct result of an investigation launched in order to uncover a non-existent evil conspiracy, a significant number of people have been found guilty of crimes they did not commit.

One of the most urgent tasks which faces the tribunal is to examine the evidence which has led to the convictions already obtained and to interrogate with the utmost scepticism the principle of what one senior police officer has called 'corroboration by volume'. Since the tribunal is not a court of appeal, and cannot overturn convictions, there can be no doubt that it will embark on this task only with extreme reluctance. This reluctance should be overcome. For a tribunal which meekly accepts its own powerlessness to assess some of the most important evidence in front of it can scarcely be said to be conducting an inquiry at all.

For the sake of all seven of the care workers from the north-west (including Cheshire and Merseyside) who continue to protest their innocence from their prison cells, *and* for the sake of those who really have been abused while in care, the tribunal should consider all the evidence which is before it, rather than a pre-selected extract from it. Only if it does this can it hope to put together the whole picture of what has happened in North Wales. After so many failed or incomplete inquiries nothing less will now suffice.

Police, Care Workers and the Creation of False Allegations

IT IS ALMOST ALWAYS extremely difficult to persuade both judges and juries that a large number of allegations of abuse which have apparently been made quite independently against a single care worker can all be false. How, if this is the case, have all these allegations come into being? While the possibility of small-scale conspiracies between two or three complainants should not be discounted, nobody could reasonably suggest that ten or fifteen complainants, sometimes from quite different parts of the country, had all managed to conspire together in order to produce a whole series of false allegations against a particular care worker. The only plausible explanation in the view of most observers (and this includes judges and juries) is that the allegations have come into existence for one very simple reason: that they are founded on fact and reflect real acts of sexual abuse which have been committed by the defendant.

But there is another possibility. It is that the allegations which have been produced by a whole series of witnesses are actually the product of the very investigation which has been designed to collect them.

The principal reason why this unusual possibility should be considered is that the kinds of police investigation which are now taking place against care workers in the north-west and elsewhere are themselves extremely unusual. These large retrospective inquiries are based on a model which has only emerged in the last ten years and which is, as yet, untested in the appeal courts; it remains fraught with dangers which have yet to be appreciated either by senior police officers or by the judiciary.

Large retrospective investigations into care homes have evolved as a response on the one hand to a growing concern among social workers about the possibility of residential abuse, and on the other hand to the the difficulty of obtaining convictions in such cases. Since sexual abuse is, almost invariably, an unwitnessed crime, and since any abuse which is alleged to have happened a long time ago will almost certainly not be reflected by medical evidence, retrospective prosecutions for abuse used to have very little chance of success; in practice, corroborating such alleged crimes was simply not possible.

Because of the dangers to innocent people of prosecuting any crime simply on the basis of the long-delayed and uncorroborated testimony of complainants, the safest course, from the point of view of justice, might have been to rule out retrospective prosecutions entirely. But during the 1990s concern about sexual abuse reached such a level that pressure was placed on police forces – and upon the Crown Prosecution Service – to find a more effective way of dealing with complaints. The task was to develop a form of investigation which would be successful in securing convictions in spite of the evidential difficulties.

The solution which was found rested on the very simple principle that convictions in retrospective cases were only likely if a number of different complainants could be found. Although different crimes would normally be tried separately in order to protect innocent defendants against the presumption of guilt, there has always been one way around this difficulty. For the law has long held that if crimes could be linked through 'striking similarities', the rules governing 'similar fact' evidence meant that these crimes could be tried together. Testimony about one alleged crime could then be offered as corroboration of another.

This approach to prosecution was fraught with dangers from the very beginning. These dangers have been significantly increased, however, by the change in the criteria for prosecuting cases involving multiple counts which has come about since 1991. Since the House of Lords decision in *DPP v. P* [1991] 2 A.C. 447 H.L. the prosecution of those against whom more than one similar offence is alleged has been made procedurally and evidentially easier. This ruling has effectively lowered the threshold for the admissibility of 'similar fact' evidence. By dispensing with the need for 'striking similarities' to undergird 'similar fact' evidence, and by allowing allegations to be linked together merely through 'similar circumstances', the 1991 ruling has actually made it much easier to secure convictions purely by advancing a sufficiently large number of uncorroborated allegations.[1]

Once these new judicial conditions began to emerge, a certain kind of police procedure was almost inevitably indicated: an initial allegation was much less likely to lead to an 'ordinary' police investigation, whereby the suspect himself would be arrested or questioned. Rather it would be treated as a signal to interview other possible complainants in order to establish whether there were further allegations against the same suspect.

In the case of alleged abuse in care homes the pool of possible complainants evidently extended to all those adults who had been in care during the period when a suspected care worker was employed. Since there was always the possibility of organised abuse, the most extensive kind of investigation into care homes would necessarily set out to trace *all* adults who had been in care during a particular period and then ensure that these potential witnesses were visited and interviewed by police officers.

Ten years ago the kind of police 'trawling' operation described here was all but unknown. But between 1988 and 1991 three large retrospective investigations were mounted into care homes in mainland Britain, all of them in the Midlands or the north-west. One of these investigations, undertaken by West Mercia Police, focused on a single private care home – Castle Hill in Ludlow, Shropshire. After extensive interviews of former residents had led to the collection of a large number of allegations, the principal of the school, Ralph Morris, was arrested and charged. Although a crucial forensic test conducted by the police proved negative, and although Morris's solicitor remains convinced to this day that some of the allegations against him were false, the weight of evidence seemed massive. In court it emerged that Morris's entire career was founded on a kind of confidence trick, that he had invented qualifications he did not have and that he had dealt dishonestly with the local authorities who sent pupils to him. Although he continued to protest his innocence throughout his trial, Morris's past behaviour effectively discredited his testimony and he was convicted. In 1996, after trying unsuccessfully to appeal against his conviction, he committed suicide in his prison cell. Whatever the truth about Morris's behaviour may have been, it seems likely that he was not guilty of some of the counts on which he was convicted.

The next major care investigation was very different. It focused on Frank Beck, a Liberal Democrat councillor and a prominent local figure, who was the first fully-qualified child-care worker ever employed by Leicestershire social services. He held positions of con-

siderable trust. In 1989, however, the suggestion was made that a
paedophile ring was being operated in the county's children's homes
and that this ring might involve not only sexual abuse but murder
and the production of snuff-films. No evidence was ever found for
the existence of any such ring but a number of allegations were collected against Beck. Although some of these were discredited during
Beck's trial, he was convicted in November 1991 on seventeen counts
of physical and sexual assault and given five life sentences.

Beck never ceased to protest his innocence and the key members
of his defence team, who believed that he was entirely innocent of the
sexual offences, succeeded in retaining Anthony Scrivener, QC, to
conduct his appeal. In 1994, however, while preparations for the
appeal were still under way, Beck died of a heart attack in prison.
Although his solicitor asked for leave from the Home Secretary to
continue his appeal posthumously, legal aid was not granted.
Because his appeal was never submitted the strength or weakness of
Beck's case will perhaps never be properly established.

*

In August 1991 an even larger retrospective investigation into care
homes was launched by the North Wales Police. The investigation
was led by Detective Superintendent Peter Ackerley, who specifically
consulted his colleagues in Leicestershire and West Mercia in order to
learn the lessons of the Beck case and the Castle Hill investigation.
Judging from the words of Detective Superintendent Ackerley
himself, it would seem that the North Wales Police saw their task as
being not simply to receive allegations but to overcome what he
described as 'the problem in terms of disclosure' by creating 'the
climate to facilitate people to tell us what went on'.[2]

In this connection it should be noted that the use of the term 'disclosure' during sexual abuse investigations was criticised in the
Butler Sloss report into the Cleveland affair, where it was pointed out
that the word implied the veracity of any allegation it was applied to.
The fact that this term, which originated in a particular social work
culture in the United States, should now commonly be used by the
police officers involved in care investigations is itself cause for
concern. For the adoption of this term tends invisibly to strengthen a
common assumption: that allegations of sexual abuse made by

former residents of care homes are likely to be true and that the primary role of the police is to collect such allegations rather than to investigate them.

One of the factors which appears to have conditioned this assumption was drawn directly from the Castle Hill investigation. During his summing up at the end of the trial of Ralph Morris on 12 April 1991, Mr Justice Fennell had said: 'I am happy that [Shropshire Social Services and West Mercia Police] will make available the experience and wisdom that has been accumulated over this trial ... and hopefully now be much more alert to these situations.' In response to these remarks Shropshire County Council eventually published *The Castle Hill Report*, which was offered as a guide to good practice in such investigations. The report contained the following advice about sexual abuse in residential establishments:

> The importance of the powerful culture within such establishments cannot be overstated when attempting to understand the inability of young men to disclose their experiences ...
>
> The identification and awareness of organised institutional abuse is still in the early stages and a significant feature of our investigation was the disbelief of other professionals and their initial inability to accept and comprehend the sheer volume and extent of the abuse. Within this setting the 'disbelief factor' exacerbated the disempowerment, vulnerability and isolation of the individual victims. It is essential, therefore, that professionals involved in this area of work be conversant with these issues, for only then can they be in a position to accept new 'systems' and take forward their practice in relation to organised abuse. *An open mind and a preparedness to accept and objectively analyse improbable and sometimes unbelievable scenarios are essential* [italics added].

Although *The Castle Hill Report* was not published until after the launch of the North Wales investigation, the ideas which informed it were already in circulation. It should be noted that these ideas included belief in widespread 'organised institutional abuse' even though the Castle Hill investigation itself involved only a single care worker and provided no evidence of any organised abuse.

The North Wales investigation was itself launched because of a suspicion that care homes in the region might have been infiltrated by an organised paedophile ring. This suspicion exerted a considerable influence not only over the 'primary' investigation which was conducted by the North Wales Police, but also, even more clearly, over the investigation, which was conducted by freelance journalist Dean Nelson on behalf of the *Independent on Sunday*. One of the questions raised by the story of North Wales is the extent to which the police investigation was in fact shaped by an even more powerful 'secondary' investigation undertaken by journalists, local politicians, social workers and others. There can be no doubt, however, that the form taken by the police investigation was influenced by ideas developed during the Castle Hill inquiry – ideas which were directly available to Superintendent Peter Ackerley through his contacts with the West Mercia Police.

The North Wales investigation was unprecedented not only because of its size but also because, before enlarging its scope to deal with care homes throughout the counties of Gwynedd and Clwyd, it originally focused on a single care home – Bryn Estyn – which had actually been closed on financial grounds seven years previously, in 1984. During the investigation more than 600 adults made allegations against no less than 365 people, most of whom were care workers from a variety of homes in North Wales. On 15 March 1992 sixteen former members of staff from Bryn Estyn were arrested at dawn. Four were charged on a number of counts of sexual abuse. Stephen Norris, who had already been convicted for offences at another home, pleaded guilty. Of the three others two were acquitted when the allegations against them were either discredited during cross-examination or shown to be medically impossible.[3] But one of them, Peter Howarth, the former deputy head of Bryn Estyn, was sentenced to ten years' imprisonment. In April 1997 Howarth, who had always protested his innocence, and who had recently instructed a new solicitor to begin work on an appeal, died of a heart attack in prison.

The North Wales investigation and the earlier investigations in Shropshire and Leicestershire were already being treated as models by other police forces. In Cheshire and in Merseyside two massive retrospective inquiries were launched in the wake of the North Wales investigation; both are still in progress. These were followed by a large operation looking into an alleged paedophile ring centred on a care home in South Wales. In August 1997 yet another huge investigation was launched in the north-east of England by the Northumbria Police, involving care homes run by five local authorities. In January 1998 the Greater Manchester Police revealed that they had opened an investigation into allegations of sexual abuse in more than seven children's homes. One of the allegations was said to date back forty years, to 1958. Many similar inquiries are already under way in other parts of the country.

Over the last five years an extremely large number of care workers have been directly affected by such investigations. Hundreds have had serious allegations made against them, and in the north-west as a whole (including North Wales, Cheshire and Merseyside) about forty have been charged with serious offences. The majority of these have been convicted and are serving sentences of up to eighteen years. The scale of the investigations undertaken in other parts of the country has yet to emerge.

It should be emphasised once again that a significant number of those convicted were indeed guilty of sexual abuse. This was true, for example, in the case of Stephen Norris, whose original conviction in 1990 served as the main trigger for the entire North Wales investigation. It was also true in the cases of Alan Langshaw and Denis Grain in Cheshire. Another man whose conduct would almost certainly have resulted in a sound conviction had he lived was the Merseyside care worker Mark Trotter, whose colleagues had raised concerns about him relatively early in his career.

But in more than a dozen cases which have already come to light, convicted care workers and teachers continue to protest their innocence. In many of these cases independent observers have examined the evidence against the convicted men and found it flawed, inconsistent or unconvincing.

*

Most of the doubts which surround these convictions arise directly from the methods of investigation used by the police. Simply because retrospective 'trawls' have been outstandingly successful in gaining convictions, this type of police inquiry has already gained acceptance both among senior police officers and in many areas of the judiciary. Yet this should not be allowed to obscure the fact that such trawls constitute, in terms of the history of policing, an extraordinary and very recent innovation. The startling nature of their departure from normal police procedure was perhaps best summed up by a senior

police officer who, when I interviewed him in 1996, pointed out that
these investigations used 'the reverse of normal police methods'. He
went on to explain that the police normally begin with an offence
which they know has been committed and set out to find out who
committed it. In the case of retrospective investigations into care
homes, however, they begin with a suspect and try to find out
whether this person has in fact committed any crime. When asked
how this object could be achieved the senior officer replied that corroboration was 'generally done by volume'. The principle relied on
was, in effect, that of 'corroboration by quantity'.

This turning upside-down of normal police methods has far-
reaching implications. Police forces normally spend their time collecting evidence in relation to crimes whose reality no one doubts.
They embark on retrospective investigations, however, without
knowing whether the crimes they are investigating have taken place
at all.

Most lay observers assume that these massive retrospective investigations are only launched in response to a large number of complaints which have been made spontaneously. In reality the opposite
is true. Almost all the retrospective investigations launched in the
last ten years have had their origin in complaints lodged by only one
or two witnesses. The vast majority of the allegations which subsequently emerge are not made spontaneously but are collected by
police officers who are actively seeking complaints against a particular suspect or against the staff of a particular home.[4]

In many cases police officers make their first contact with potential witnesses by tracing their address and then literally knocking on
their door. They will then ask them about their time in care. They
may ask specifically about whether they have complaints or whether
they were ever abused. Sometimes officers will follow up the initial
visit, during which their readiness to receive allegations is often
apparent, with a second visit a few days later, during which they take
a statement. It sometimes happens that witnesses who say at first
that they have no complaints make allegations during this second
visit. Such contradictory testimony is usually treated as a sign that
the alleged abuse was real and that it was difficult to 'disclose' earlier
because of fear or embarrassment. An alternative explanation is that
preliminary visits by the police may actually serve to sow the seeds
of false allegations which are subsequently harvested. In many cases

the witnesses in question may still be in touch with others who were at the same care home, and there is always the possibility that the interval between police visits may be used to compare notes and dovetail allegations.

The seeds of false allegations can also be inadvertently planted in other ways. In some retrospective investigations the initial contact with witnesses is made in a letter in which they are invited to complain about abuse they may have suffered during their time in care. In September 1997 former residents of St George's School in Formby, Merseyside, received the following letter from Detective Superintendent John Robbins of the Merseyside Police:

Dear ....

OPERATION CARE

I am the senior investigating officer of the above operation which is currently investigating allegations of child abuse reported to have taken place within a number of residential establishments in the Merseyside area.

I am aware from records provided to me that in times past you have been a resident at St George's/Clarence House School situated in the Formby area of Merseyside, whilst in the care of a local authority. I am concerned that there is a possibility that such abuse may have taken place whilst you were in residence there.

If you have any information or if we can help you with any complaint you may have, please respond by completing and returning the attached slip using the enclosed pre-paid envelope or by contacting a member of my staff using the above telephone number.

MAY I TAKE THIS OPPORTUNITY OF ASSURING YOU THAT ANY INFORMATION GIVEN OR COMPLAINT MADE WILL BE TREATED IN THE STRICTEST CONFIDENCE.

If you do not wish to communicate with the Police or Social Services at this time, but feel you would like to discuss any events which have taken place, you may wish to use the independent and confidential counselling service offered by BARNARDOS COUNSELLING 0151–707–1327. If they cannot assist I am sure they can put you in touch with a counselling service which can.

Please reply by 25th September 1997.

Thank you for your assistance in this matter.

Yours faithfully,

J. H. Robbins
Detective Superintendent

The reference to a counselling service is now a standard part of police procedure in care investigations. Because the recollection of sexual abuse can be deeply distressing, investigating officers routinely give out the number of a telephone helpline or counselling service. It is relatively common for former residents who have not made complaints to the police to piece together allegations during counselling sessions given by therapists or during meetings with probation officers. Alternatively some complaints which have initially been made to the police are greatly elaborated during the counselling which sometimes follows. This happened, for example, throughout the Bryn Estyn investigation, when massive local and national publicity was given to a helpline staffed by NSPCC counsellors. In this case, as in most others, the helpline was actively promoted by the police force involved in the investigation. As well as encouraging potential complainants to use helplines, police officers frequently make use of local and national news media in order to publicise investigations which have just been launched. Such police forays are perhaps best characterised as 'begging-bowl operations'. Their central purpose is to alleviate the poverty of the initial evidence against a suspect by collecting large numbers of complaints against him which might not otherwise have been made.

*

Any operation in which police officers are actively seeking fresh allegations against a particular suspect or institution is intrinsically dangerous. Investigations into care homes, however, are doubly dangerous. This is because such investigations, by necessity, involve a very unusual pool of witnesses.

Although these witnesses are frequently referred to as former residents of 'children's homes', this term is misleading. Most retrospective investigations have focused not on children's homes but on institutions which deal with difficult or disturbed adolescents, some of whom have been in trouble with the police. The former residents of such institutions are often both emotionally damaged and economically disadvantaged. A large proportion have criminal convictions and some are highly suggestible. Many have deep, and often well-founded resentments against 'the system'. When they find that police officers are actually offering to help them make a particular kind of complaint, they may well be tempted to substitute a fictitious allegation of sexual or physical abuse for a real but general resentment which they feel.

This temptation is almost certain to be strengthened by the deep feelings of powerlessness and rejection which are felt by many who have spent their adolescence in care homes. They may now find that they are valued and sympathetically attended to by police officers, counsellors and social workers *according to the seriousness of the abuse which they allege.* The power of accusation is in this respect huge and there are many damaged and emotionally vulnerable people who find that this power, once tasted, proves intoxicating.

Such people may find it relatively easy to make false allegations against those who once cared for them precisely because they have themselves come from troubled family backgrounds. They may have been treated badly, or even rejected, by the very people who at other times have cared for them most – their own parents. They may even find it psychologically difficult to conceive of a caring figure who is not, simultaneously, in some sense, an abuser. Perhaps more importantly still they may make a false allegation against a care worker precisely because they have been led to believe that there is already evidence that this person is guilty. One of the ways in which they may seek to justify fabricating evidence is by persuading themselves that they are engaged in a battle against evil. To participate in such a battle can be psychologically energising and can give both meaning and purpose to people whose lives may have lacked both.

The belief of social workers and counsellors that it is actually therapeutic to bring out as many memories of abuse as possible now appears to have been transferred to some police officers, and this may actually put pressure on some witnesses to make more and more allegations. The kind of subtle pressure involved is perceptively described by Jean La Fontaine in her recent book about satanic abuse allegations:

> Sympathetic acceptance of a story slides easily into a curiosity to learn more. When the listener is eager to hear more, gratitude for support may impel the young person to … find ever more dramatic memories to recount. This approach to abuse gives no indication of how to tell when the account has ended; the victim's claim to have no more to tell may not be accepted but be interpreted as a refusal to tell something even worse than what has already been recounted.[5]

The suggestibility of many witnesses in care investigations, however, is not simply due to psychological factors. It is also financially conditioned. During the past twenty years an entire sub-culture of compensation-seeking has grown up among prison inmates and those who are part of a criminal culture. Exceptionally large payments, sometimes totalling more than £100,000, have been made in some civil cases associated with sexual abuse, notably the Frank Beck case. The Criminal Injuries Compensation Board has also made smaller but still substantial payments in similar cases. Many former residents of care homes are aware of the fact that such payments are possible. In such circumstances, the psychological suggestibility of witnesses is strongly reinforced by the financial incentive to make false allegations.

In one or two cases witnesses have come forward to confirm that allegations have been deliberately fabricated. One of the cases in the north-west involved an elaborate allegation made against Anthony Joiner, a care worker, by former resident Kevin Mutford.* In this particular case the solicitor acting for Joiner was able to locate another ex-resident who pointed to a number of improbabilities in Mutford's allegation. He went further than this, however:

> I met Kevin Mutford in prison about two months ago … I asked him why he was making such accusations about Mr Joiner. Kevin said 'I'M JUST AFTER THE MONEY. YOU SHOULD TRY IT YOURSELF.' I told him that although I did not get on well with Mr Joiner to begin with I wouldn't go to a court and lie over something like that. He, again, said he was doing it for the money and that what he said against Mr Joiner was a load of nonsense.

* The names of this care worker and of all witnesses in this and other cases have been changed.

Another example of the compensation-motive at work emerged during the proceedings of the North Wales Tribunal. It was pointed out that one particular complainant, Ray Slingby, had made very serious allegations against John Allen, the proprietor of the privately run Bryn Alyn care home, and had then made a claim to the Criminal Injuries Compensation Authority. Allen was subsequently convicted on the basis of allegations made by other complainants. But the police established that Slingby had never even been in residence at Bryn Alyn. When threatened with prosecution for wasting police time he immediately withdrew his allegation. In the police interview which ensued he explained that he had made a false allegation partly in order to 'get at' John Allen and partly in order to claim compensation.

Although it is by no means the only factor involved, and although psychological factors are crucial, the potency of the compensation-motive should not be underestimated. An individual may sometimes go to painful lengths in order to claim compensation. One of the complainants in the case of Roy Shuttleworth, actually had a previous conviction for conspiring with a friend to gain money by deception from the Criminal Injuries Compensation Board. He had deliberately inflicted a knife-wound on his accomplice's back which was so serious that it needed 102 stitches. Shuttleworth, however, was convicted partly on the basis of this complainant's testimony and is now serving ten years in prison.

*

Both the financial vulnerability and the psychological suggestibility of the witnesses in these cases become even more significant when we recognise that police officers do not play merely a passive or neutral role in the kind of investigation which is under consideration. Once the police operation has been initiated, either by a single allegation or by a mere suspicion, police officers who go on to interview other possible witnesses will be actively seeking similar allegations and may, in spite of all their best intentions, actually intimate to their witnesses the kinds of allegation they are looking for. This they may do either by asking leading questions which include the names of suspects, or by dropping hints without even realising what they are doing.

Once police officers have become convinced that a particular individual is guilty of abuse it becomes very difficult to avoid communicating their own feelings of certainty to those they are interviewing. One example of this has been provided by a witness in the North Wales investigation, John Holmes. According to Holmes, when police officers visited him *they* told *him* that he had been sexually abused at Bryn Estyn. They then named the man who had suppos-edly abused him – Peter Howarth. Holmes says that when he pointed out that this abuse had never taken place the police officers made it clear that he would be eligible for compensation if he alleged abuse. At this point he asked them to leave.

The experience of John Holmes may be compared with that of another witness in the North Wales investigation, who wrote the fol-lowing in a letter to a solicitor:

> ... as to the child abuse case in Bryn Estyn School, when the police from North Wales took a statement at my address, they told me, if I was abused, I would get money in compensation, I was just dumbfounded when he came out with it, I feel ... that most people thought they would get compensation just saying it, that's why most people have come forward, trying to make a quick buck out of the system. I feel the police [put] pressure on people to come forward saying you get compensation.

These examples, in which police officers appear to be exercising a powerful and obvious influence on potential witnesses, may seem to call into question the integrity of the officers involved. But any sug-gestion that police officers have set out deliberately to fabricate evi-dence in these cases would almost certainly be wrong. Perhaps the best analogy is provided by the bee that moves from flower to flower collecting nectar. The bee, which is only going about its business, does not for one moment suspect that it may actually be pollinating the flower in the very act of visiting it. And the bee certainly has no conception that the entire garden which is in bloom around it is only in existence at all because bees have been busy carrying pollen from one flower to another summer after summer for many years.

So it is with some police investigations. While there are indeed inquiries into residential abuse where the allegations are well-founded, there are other investigations which appear to have grown entirely out of an atmosphere of suspicion, or out of a single unsub-stantiated allegation.

Sometimes, as can be seen from the examples given above, the role of police officers in shaping the evidence which they collect is both direct and obvious to an outside observer. Even more dangerous, however, are the more subtle forms of influence which can be exercised. Perhaps the most important area here is the method of questioning which is used. Even though police officers may be given strict instructions to avoid asking leading questions, such instructions are, in practice, enormously difficult to comply with. Leading questions are among the most common of all interviewing techniques, and they tend to be used automatically in situations where people are trying to coax information from informants who are thought to be inhibited by shame or anxiety. Most people are simply not aware of how frequently they employ such questions, and even well-trained police officers sometimes use them without realising it.

This is particularly likely to happen in retrospective investigations where witnesses are being asked questions about a period in their life which they may only dimly remember. In such circumstances it is only natural for the investigating officers to try to jog their memory by mentioning certain characteristics of the care home in question. Alternatively they may try to help them remember an individual care worker by describing a particular activity he used regularly to engage in. Precisely because this approach is likely to be effective in eliciting genuine memories, police officers may not recognise how dangerous it is. In most cases they will not understand that they are actually holding out to the witness, who may already have both a psychological and a financial motive to fabricate evidence, a template for the very allegation they are seeking. When an allegation is then made, either on the original visit, or on some subsequent visit, they may actually fail to recognise that they have themselves suggested it.

It is in this way that a police force, conscientiously investigating suspicions which it has been encouraged to entertain about a particular individual, may actually succeed in bringing into being an entire series of false allegations. It is then almost inevitable that, unless this process is pointed out during the trial, the innocent care worker in question will be convicted. This is because nobody, unless they had studied the investigative process closely, would ever dream that a series of allegations which have apparently been made quite independently, might have its origins not in memories of real acts of abuse, but in the suspicions entertained, and the suggestions inadvertently made by investigating officers.

To characterise a police investigation in this way is not entirely without precedent. Writing in 1991 about police methods in general, McConville, Sanders and Leng suggested that it is normal for police to play an active part in shaping the statements of those they are interviewing, particularly when they have become intent on a prosecution: 'Whilst verballing, etc., may be an extreme form of behaviour, police work is systemically geared to the construction of evidence: the creation of evidence in one way or another is not a deviant police act but a standard form of production. The processes of production are more subtle and complex than "verballing" suggests, and more easily overlooked, but they are all-pervasive.' Elsewhere the same writers suggest that interrogations are best understood as social encounters 'fashioned to confirm and legitimate a police narrative'.[6]

Although these remarks are intended by their authors to apply primarily to the interrogation of suspects, the habit of mind they describe can very easily be transferred to the interviewing of witnesses. To the extent that the statements made have actually been shaped by the police officers who have conducted the interview (either through leading questions or through the unintentional misreporting of witnesses' words), to that same extent will they tend to confirm and substantiate the original police narrative. In investigations where the pool of witnesses is fundamentally honest, the natural tendency of police officers to seek to consolidate the power of their own narrative, even where it conflicts with the truth, will be opposed continually. But in investigations where the witnesses, or some of them, have much to gain by accepting a false police narrative, the process of 'investigation' may actually come to resemble the writing of fiction. Provided that the original police narrative is powerful enough, each new witness will serve only to strengthen it further, while simultaneously disguising its true origins. Without even recognising what they are doing, police officers may actually end up by 'creating' a significant proportion of the evidence they believe they are merely uncovering. Because it has now become relatively easy to accumulate a large number of false allegations against any care worker who has fallen under suspicion the situation which has resulted is fraught with danger for all care workers. What the police have inadvertently created is a machine for bringing about miscarriages of justice.

*

The idea that allegations might actually be unintentionally created by those who investigate suspicions of sexual abuse is not a new one. When a group of parents in Rochdale were accused of satanic ritual abuse in 1989, a study undertaken by an expert witness revealed that the allegations had been unwittingly constructed by the very team of investigators who had interviewed the children. A very similar conclusion was reached in relation to allegations of satanic abuse which were made shortly before in the Nottingham Broxtowe case.

When Nottingham police and social workers reached deadlock over this investigation in 1989, the Chief Constable of Nottingham and the Director of Social Services for Nottinghamshire commissioned a report from a Joint Enquiry Team made up of police officers and social workers. This team eventually produced what became known as the Nottingham JET report. It concluded that the allegations of satanic abuse, though ostensibly made independently by those who were claiming to be victims, had actually been sown by the social workers investigating the case. In the view of the Joint Enquiry Team, the entire case demonstrated 'how evidence can, for want of a better term, be "created". This is to say you start with nothing except your own beliefs and end up with the story that you expected and wanted to hear before you started.'[7]

The Joint Enquiry Team report went on to suggest that parts of the Social Services Department appeared to have developed an 'unshakeable' belief in satanic ritual abuse through which they were unwittingly encouraging children to allege bizarre acts of abuse which had never taken place. 'This could lead eventually', the report concluded, 'to grave injustice, and, if unchecked, it has the ingredients of a modern "witch-hunt".' In the view of the team all the elements necessary to such a witch-hunt were already present. These included 'rigid, preconceived ideas, dubious investigative techniques, the unwillingness to check basic facts'.

In a telling and, it would seem, prophetic passage, the 1990 report noted that 'Recently claims have been made in the social work press that sexual abuse is occurring in 75% or even 100% of the nation's children's homes and the same report considered ritual abuse in this context ... If this country followed the precedent of the USA the next step would be extensive allegations of ritual/Satanic and sexual abuse against residential and day care workers.'

Such allegations have now surfaced, and nowhere more so than in the county of Cheshire in an investigation which has been profoundly influenced by a number of Cheshire social workers. In this respect it should perhaps be noted that in 1987 Cheshire social workers were involved in the investigation of what appears to have been the very first alleged case of satanic abuse in Britain at Congleton. Their willingness in that context to credit bizarre (and untrue) 'disclosures' coaxed out of young children during therapy was commented on by the authors of the JET report.[8]

It should also be noted that one of the outside consultants to the Cheshire investigation was himself once an enthusiastic believer in satanic abuse. Former probation officer Ray Wyre, who was specifically criticised in the JET report, was commissioned by the Cheshire Police in 1996 to mount a training session for police officers, barristers and solicitors involved in the Cheshire investigation.[9] In September 1996 two child protection officers from the Cheshire Police actually conducted a workshop at a conference held by the Ritual Abuse Information Network Support (RAINS), an organisation which has in the past credulously and repeatedly propagated belief in the idea of organised ritual abuse carried out by satanic cults.

Organised ritual abuse by non-existent satanic cults and sexual abuse in residential care are not, of course, the same phenomena. Nobody is suggesting that sexual abuse does not sometimes take place in residential care. Once again it needs to be stressed that some of those who have already been convicted for such offences are clearly guilty. But there is a very grave danger that a number of real and very serious offences committed in children's homes during the past twenty or thirty years may become the basis of a moral panic and a new witch-hunt of exactly the kind which was predicted in the report of the Nottingham Joint Enquiry Team. Indeed the bitter reality, it would seem, is that we are already in the midst of just such a witch-hunt.

The only way to protect innocent residential workers against the kind of false allegations which now appear to be proliferating is to introduce new legislation. Such legislation should proscribe the kind of trawling operations which are currently being used by police forces throughout the country, and outlaw the practice of advertising or appealing for allegations which is now commonly engaged in not only by police forces, but by some journalists, solicitors and others. It should also introduce a time-limit on the bringing of proceedings so that innocent men may have a reasonable chance of preparing their defence against false allegations. Such measures are essential if we are to protect care workers and others against the possibility of grave injustice. For only if investigations are undertaken in a quite different manner, and in a quite different spirit, will it be possible to ensure that allegations are not spread inadvertently by precisely that process of suggestion and cross-pollination which is so common in investigations into alleged sexual abuse.

Where wisdom prevails it seems possible that appropriate action will be taken as a matter of urgency by the individual chief constables of forces where retrospective investigations into care homes are already in progress. But wisdom does not always prevail. For this reason it is extremely important that the issue is not left solely to the discretion of chief constables and that it is dealt with by legislation. The kind of safeguards indicated here should be introduced not simply in order to protect innocent care workers, but to protect the integrity of the justice system itself. For in any investigation where the goal of securing convictions becomes more important than that of securing justice, justice itself is undermined.

Until such safeguards are adopted there is a great danger that the sincere zeal of social workers and police officers to uncover what they believe to be real crimes will actually lead them to discover imaginary crimes and to send innocent men to prison for committing these crimes.

Too many innocent men have been sent to prison already. If we do not both acknowledge and call a halt to one of the most dangerous developments in methods of police investigation which has ever taken place, many more are likely to join them.

The Great Children's Home Panic

THE IDEA THAT CHILDREN'S HOMES have been infiltrated by an evil conspiracy of paedophiles is relatively recent. But the general notion that there exists an evil conspiracy which is given to preying on innocent children and causing them harm is an ancient one. In the past this notion has taken many forms – among them the accusation of ritual murder traditionally levelled by Christians against Jews during the days leading up to Good Friday. First made in Norwich in 1144, the accusation usually took the form of a baseless claim that a group of Jews had kidnapped a Christian child and tortured or murdered it for ritual purposes. This blood libel circled the globe and travelled down the centuries to the time of Hitler, establishing itself in the process as one of the main motifs of Christian and post-Christian anti-semitism. The sinister conspiracy of child-murdering Jews to which it pointed was a figment of the Christian imagination, but this did not prevent countless innocent Jewish people from being hunted down and killed in the name of justice and of Christian virtue.

A comparable fantasy which for a time was to prove even more compelling to the Christian imagination was that which maintained the existence of a society of witches who flew through the air astride rams, pigs or broomsticks and gathered together to engage in the orgiastic worship of their master, Satan. The members of this evil conspiracy supposedly took particular delight in besmirching that which was holy and destroying innocence. They were sometimes imagined killing and eating young children or babies in sacrificial rituals.

In Britain and America the most lurid versions of this fantasy had virtually no currency. But in continental Europe the fantasy was sometimes worked out in extraordinary and vivid sexual detail. The handbooks of witch-finders and the testimony of those whom they forced to confess often had an overtly erotic or obscene character. They became, in effect, a body of legitimate pornography for an educated elite consisting of bishops, ministers, magistrates and judges. By turns fascinated and horrified by its vivid sexual content, many of those who heard evidence of witchcraft suspended their critical judgement. They unsceptically accepted accounts of crimes which were unlikely or impossible and came to believe unreservedly in the reality of an evil conspiracy which did not exist. As a result countless innocent men and women were convicted of offences they had never committed and many were executed or burned alive.

Some twenty years ago a new form of testimony, which initially seemed to bear no resemblance to the fantasies which had enthralled our zealous Christian forebears, began to fascinate courtrooms in America and Europe. It emerged when social workers and therapists began to focus their most urgent attention on the crime of child sexual abuse.

It was in California in the 1970s and 1980s that a new culture of child protection gradually emerged. One of the influences which lay behind this development was the emergence of radical feminist theories of patriarchy and of the manner in which patriarchal authority was supposedly maintained. In a feminist conference which took place in New York in 1971 the social worker Florence Rush put forward her view that child sexual abuse was deliberately permitted by patriarchal societies, and clearly implied that it was the cornerstone of patriarchal authority:

> Sexual abuse of children is permitted because it is an unspoken but prominent factor in socializing and preparing the female to accept a subordinate role: to feel guilty, ashamed and to tolerate through fear, the power exercised over her by men ... The female's early sexual experiences prepare her to submit in later life to the adult forms of sexual abuse heaped on her by her boyfriend, her lover, her husband. In short the sexual abuse of female children is a process of education that prepares them to become the wives and mothers of America.[10]

These words powerfully convey the outrage of many women at the *real* subordination they suffer at the hands of men. Largely because they contain an element of truth, their distorted view of child sexual abuse as having been virtually institutionalised by patriarchy was often accepted uncritically by feminist thinkers in the 1970s. It was this approach to sexual abuse which helped to promote interest in the early views of Freud. Florence Rush herself was one of the pioneers in formulating the idea that Freud had recognised the role of child sexual abuse in causing neurosis, but had backed away from his 'discovery' out of cowardice. After 1977, when Rush published a version of this idea in the first issue of the feminist journal *Chrysalis*, the attitudes of mental health professionals towards the entire subject of sexual abuse began to be coloured by this view. This was particularly true in California, where a powerful grouping of therapists, social workers and feminists developed a new approach to child sexual abuse.[11]

One of the distinctive features of the new therapeutic approach which gradually emerged in California was the manner in which it set out to combat the systematic disbelief with which allegations of sexual abuse were all too frequently met. The development was in many respects both necessary and overdue. But the rigid ideology which lay behind this view meant that in too many cases an attitude of systematic disbelief was replaced not by an open-minded willingness to investigate, but by a kind of systematic credulity. In the new Californian model of child protection it thus gradually became an article of faith among social workers and therapists that children did not make false allegations about sexual abuse. As early as 1978 this new feminist view was noted approvingly by Roland Summit, the Los Angeles County mental health consultant who rapidly came to regard himself, and to be regarded by his fellow professionals, as one of the leading authorities on child sexual abuse. 'It has become a maxim among child sexual abuse intervention counsellors and investigators,' wrote Summit approvingly, 'that children never fabricate the kinds of explicit sexual manipulations they divulge in complaints and interrogations.' His own view was that children should always be believed, no matter how unlikely their accusations: 'The more illogical and incredible the initiation scene might seem to adults, the more likely it is that the child's description is valid.' This kind of faith in the accuracy of children's statements about sexual abuse, was, in Summit's view, a necessary doctrine for all who worked in the field of child-care, and only if it was embraced unreservedly could society be cured of one of its most dangerous ills. In the crusading paper in which he announced this belief he also described a disturbing pattern of behaviour by observing how frequently daughters who had accused their father of incest went on to retract their allegations in order to avoid breaking up the family. Summit's paper, 'The Child Sexual Abuse Accommodation Syndrome', would remain unpublished for another five years. In the meantime, however, it was widely circulated in manuscript and came to be treated, even before it was published, as one of the informal 'scriptures' of modern child protection professionals in America.[12]

It should immediately be said that Summit's influential paper did contain significant elements of truth. There can be no doubt that daughters who are the victims of incest *do* sometimes withdraw well-founded allegations. They may do this because they have been pressurised by one or both of their parents, or because they recognise that their allegations might lead to the breaking-up of the entire family. It is also the case that, when sexually unsophisticated children *spontaneously* make detailed and realistic claims about being sexually abused by adults, they are quite likely to be telling the truth. One of the reasons for saying this is that such children simply may not possess the kind of knowledge which is necessary to construct *plausible* narratives about sexual assault. There can therefore be little doubt that the reforms introduced in California did lead in many cases, especially in the early years, to a more sensitive and realistic attitude to allegations which proceeded directly from children.

It was perhaps for this reason that the Californian model was officially adopted by the American National Council for Child Abuse and Neglect in 1979, and used as the basis for a national training programme. It was at this point, as anxieties about incest and child sexual abuse began to rise to unprecedented levels, that the inherent dangers of the Californian approach began to emerge.

What the pioneers of the new approach had ignored is something that many sensitive and experienced lawyers and psychologists have long recognised: young children, while certainly not inherently untruthful, can sometimes be unreliable witnesses. This is because children often find it even more difficult than adults to distinguish between fact and fantasy. At the same time they are particularly vulnerable to suggestion and, simply because of their relative powerlessness, are prone to construct narratives on the basis of what they believe parents, social workers, therapists or other authority-figures want to hear. Sometimes they recognise these confabulations as 'stories'. Quite frequently, however, they actually come to believe in their essential truth, and they may present them as historical fact with utter sincerity, even under questioning.[13]

As the Californian model and derivatives of it began to be adopted on a nationwide scale throughout America, the phrase which was most frequently to be heard on the lips of social workers and therapists was 'Believe the children!' These words, indeed, became the informal and immensely powerful slogan of the entire exercise in consciousness-raising which was undertaken by campaigning feminists and child protection workers throughout the 1970s and the 1980s. The great irony was that, in many inquiries into cases of alleged sexual abuse, the children involved could sometimes be neither seen nor heard by the law enforcement officers who were actually investigating. Instead these children were closeted with other adults and were allowed to tell their stories only after they had been subjected to pressure and repeated suggestive questioning. In an alarming number of cases children's repeated and honest denials that anything untoward had happened were routinely and aggressively *disbelieved*. Only when they began to construct stories which accorded with what adults had suspected or alleged did they find that they were indeed believed.

In some instances social workers and therapists were undoubtedly able to carry out faithfully their promise that they would 'believe the children'. In all too many cases, however, this slogan actually became a beguiling and powerful way of secreting a much older view in the very heart of the child protection profession. For the shibboleth which best reflected the new Californian *practice*, as opposed to its idealistic theory, was both deeply traditional *and* patriarchal. It was nothing other than 'The adults know best'.

It was this immensely powerful Californian model, with its ideological taboo against disbelieving any allegation of sexual abuse, however improbable, which would profoundly influence child protection work not only in America but throughout the English-speaking world.

*

Once child sexual abuse had been redefined not simply as a social ill, which it undoubtedly was and is, but as the supreme evil of our age, it was perhaps inevitable that ancient demonological fantasies would be mobilised once again.

Throughout the early 1980s a particular fantasy began to grip the imagination of an influential grouping of child protection workers who had been trained in the new climate of credulity. This fantasy, which initially gained currency in California, maintained that small children, usually in pre-school nurseries, were being systematically preyed on by an organised conspiracy of adults who belonged to a satanic sexual cult. A complex set of beliefs associated with this fantasy, in which the existence of highly organised satanic cults dedicated to the sexual abuse and sacrifice of young children was taken for granted, now rapidly spread throughout the United States. It was then introduced to child protection workers in Britain and elsewhere so that by the early 1990s it had achieved a significant currency in many parts of the English-speaking world.[14]

For a number of child protection workers, unqualified belief in this new and powerful fantasy became a kind of religious faith. So complete was their dedication to the crusade against the forces of evil they could not even consider the possibility that the evil conspiracies they had come to believe in might not, in fact, exist at all. They certainly never suspected that in some cases they had themselves created the 'disclosures' which they attributed to children or that that their fight against 'evil' might lead to the conviction of innocent people. Yet in countless tragic cases, both in the United States and elsewhere, this is what happened. The members of a movement which had set out to combat a real social ill – child sexual abuse – had become so consumed by a crusade against what had come to be seen as the supreme evil that they sometimes ended by abusing innocent children and innocent parents themselves.*

There can be no doubt at all that the new intensified awareness of child sexual abuse which came with the Californian model did bring some benefits to a number of vulnerable children who had suffered sexual abuse. But the deployment of enormous human and financial resources in the investigation of a large number of imaginary instances of sexual abuse actually bled resources from work which

---

* It is commonly believed that the various satanic scares in Britain did not lead to any convictions. This is not the case. In June 1994 in Pembroke, west Wales, the largest trial for organised child sexual abuse ever to have taken place in Britain came to an end, with six men receiving prison sentences totalling fifty-three years. Although the case eventually involved allegations against as many as 200 people, and although these allegations involved many of the usual features of satanic scares, social workers and police were careful to downplay both the size of the supposed conspiracy and the satanic elements, and this undoubtedly helped to secure the convictions.

might have prevented the abuse of children or which dealt with genuine cases of abuse. At the same time the new vigilance of social workers and other professionals all too frequently engendered a culture of suspicion which fuelled the increase in false allegations.

By 1990 the crisis produced by the spread of false allegations began to grow to acute proportions, particularly in America. So grave were the tragedies caused in America by such phenomena as the McMartin day care case, and in Britain by satanic scares such as those in Nottingham, Rochdale and the Orkneys, that the first concerted opposition began to emerge. In Britain scepticism about satanic abuse first emerged during the Nottingham case, where police officers investigating allegations of ritual abuse could find no supporting evidence (see above, pp. 31–32). A more general scepticism about allegations of satanic abuse was first expressed in the *Independent on Sunday* and it was subsequently taken up by other publications, including *Private Eye*. When journalists ridiculed the belief in organised satanic cults as a delusion and pointed out that 'investigations have produced no bodies, no bones, no bloodstains, nothing', some believers resisted fiercely. Even today, almost ten years after stories of satanic abuse were effectively discredited, a surprising number of social workers and therapists find it difficult to accept that an entire profession once came close to embracing a delusion. Many cling resolutely to their belief that organised satanic abuse is a real phenomenon.[15]

Yet, largely because of the hostility shown both by police forces and by journalists towards such allegations, those who continued to believe in organised satanic abuse were rendered effectively powerless. Without the support of journalists they could not maintain the support of the public and without the support of the police they could never hope to secure the convictions they sought.

From about 1990 onwards, however, a number of those who had been zealous believers in satanic abuse began to adapt their beliefs to the climate of scepticism which had grown up around their wilder claims. From a pragmatic point of view such willingness to adapt had become a necessity if they were to retain credibility and influence within the larger community of social workers and therapists, many of whom did not share their extremism. The problem for conspiracy theorists was, in a sense, one of evolutionary survival; the task was to find the particular kind of conspiracy theory most likely to survive in an environment of police scepticism and resistance on the part of both the press and the public.

One of the developments which exercised a considerable influence over this evolutionary process was the gradual discrediting of the term 'satanic abuse' and its replacement by the much more sober label of 'organised abuse'. This label emerged as a diplomatic compromise which could be applied *both* to real or imaginary paedophile rings *and* to cases where satanic abuse by organised cults was alleged. Its use was supported both by the British Association of Social Workers and by the Department of Health in its guidelines for child protection workers, *Working Together*, issued in response to the Cleveland affair. 'By using a neutral term,' Jean La Fontaine has written, 'both organisations hoped to avoid a damaging split in their ranks between those who believed the allegations of "satanic" or "ritual abuse" and those who did not.'[16]

The emergence of this term meant in practice that social workers' beliefs about paedophile rings evolved in an environment which was profoundly influenced by the conspiracy theories of believers in satanic cults. There was also, however, strong pressure to 'desatanise' conspiracy theories and effectively secularise them. In addition to this there was another very important factor. For, as is implied by the title of the guidelines it issued, the reaction of the Department of Health to the Cleveland affair had been to encourage different agencies – and above all social workers and the police – to work much more closely together. Although a number of influential social workers had developed a profound and bitter hostility to the traditional patriarchalism of police culture, institutional pressures and government guidelines meant that they had no realistic option but to work closely with the police. In these circumstances there was almost bound to be some kind of accommodation between the culture of the police and the culture of social work.

It was in these conditions that, alongside the discredited notion of organised satanic conspiracies, there rapidly grew up the much more plausible belief that certain children's homes had actually been taken over by paedophile rings, and were being managed by well-organised networks of abusers.

During the investigation into Frank Beck, which took place at the same time as the Nottingham satanic scare, the notion that organised paedophile rings had already infiltrated some children's homes began to grip the imagination of a number of social workers and child protection professionals in very much the same way as satanic conspiracy theories had done previously. This new conspiracy theory rapidly became established within the culture of social work and a number of those who had previously exercised their vigilance in seeking signs of satanic conspiracies now anxiously looked for evidence of this new phenomenon. What was perhaps even more important was that senior police officers, who had been so resistant to the idea of organised satanic cults, were sometimes prepared to consider this possibility.

One reason for this was that after the disastrous breakdown in relationships between social workers and police which had taken place in Cleveland and in Nottingham, some police officers had much more contact with the field of child protection. Assumptions which had gained ground in this field were no longer being imposed from without by antagonistic social workers, and some police forces set up child protection units of their own. The officers involved in these units were gradually inducted into the emerging culture of child protection. They found themselves participating in seminars and training sessions whose powerful sexual content sometimes served to mask the unsoundness of the ideas which were propagated in them. In these new circumstances some police officers began to absorb elements of the Californian model and to employ the vocabulary of child protection professionals. In some cases they too learned to regard complaints of sexual abuse not as allegations to be investigated but as 'disclosures' to be accepted.

The idea that children's homes had been infiltrated by paedophiles was a beguiling one for many police officers. It appealed both to their genuine concern about vulnerable children and to the homophobia which has always been a powerful element in police culture. What added to the psychological appeal of this idea was that the kind of investigation it demanded usually involved adults rather than children. This being so, officers were able to interview potential complainants without social workers being present. Male police officers could therefore reassure themselves that, although they were in theory dealing with allegations of sexual abuse against children, they were really doing 'a man's job'.

One crucial result of this new development was that it effectively hid from police officers the possibility that the evidence they were now collecting might itself be contaminated. In Cleveland and

Nottingham the ideological conflict between police and social workers had sharpened the critical faculties of the police, and led them to examine social workers' methods with more than ordinary care. In the early retrospective investigations into care homes, however, police officers themselves were responsible for collecting the larger part of the evidence. Lacking any objective perspective on their own techniques of questioning, they were unable to regard them with proper scepticism; their own tendency to contaminate the evidence they were collecting became effectively invisible to them.

Even in these hazardous conditions, however, a measure of empiricism survived; the police officers who have been involved in retrospective investigations have not yet either discovered or 'created' evidence of the existence of organised paedophile rings in children's homes. In terms of its evidential backing, this theory seems, so far at least, to belong just as much to the realms of fantasy as the one it has effectively displaced. To their credit the senior police officers who led the massive investigations in the north-west have not sought to conceal this fact and have proclaimed it in public. But few observers have faced up to the implications of their words. Nor it must be said, have the police officers themselves. The main reason for this is that the investigations triggered by the new conspiracy theory *have* been remarkably 'successful' in collecting a very large number of allegations of abuse. They have also been successful in a way that the old satanic theory rarely was. For, as we have seen, retrospective investigations have already led to a large number of convictions. In a police culture which has been impoverished by the pressure of crude law-and-order politics, so that convictions (and the length of the sentences handed down) have become almost the sole measure of success, this has proved decisive. Simply because of their effectiveness at obtaining convictions, deeply flawed methods of investigation have been tolerated or even championed by senior police officers. These methods are rapidly spreading to other police forces throughout the country largely because they have already led to an unprecedented number of convictions involving prison sentences of up to eighteen years.

*

The full story of how our perception of 'children's homes' has been changed over the past ten years, a story which is both fascinating and disturbing, cannot be told in detail here. It should be noted, however, that the paedophile-ring theory of children's homes originally developed and gathered strength – as had earlier ideas about satanic abuse – in the minds of a relatively small number of social workers and child protection professionals. Just as the early satanic rumours in Britain were lent considerable support by the NSPCC, so too was the more recent panic about children's homes.[17] Only when the idea had been tested and developed within the field of child protection was it passed on to police forces. Only at the point where some police forces were already beginning to become sceptical about it was it disseminated to a wider public.

The chief agents of this process of dissemination were journalists. In December 1991 the *Independent on Sunday* was responsible for breaking the story of North Wales in a sensational front-page report in which it lent its own well-earned authority to a claim which can only be described as extraordinary. Its report suggested that children's homes throughout North Wales had been infiltrated by an organised paedophile ring which included police officers and which was therefore being covered up by the very police force charged with the task of investigating it. This idea was subsequently taken up both by *Private Eye*, which discovered a malign Masonic conspiracy in the heart of North Wales, and by the *Observer*, which claimed in a headline that no less than twelve police officers were part of a 'paedophile ring' supposedly operating in North Wales children's homes. The very newspapers which had successfully poured cold water on the satanic abuse scares and helped to extinguish their fires were now eagerly fanning the flames of a new conflagration which was potentially even more dangerous.[18]

It was not until 1996, however, that the scare about children's homes was turned into a full-scale moral panic. The event which led to this was the decision taken by Clwyd County Council to refrain from publishing a report into the North Wales allegations which had been produced by three child-care experts. This report had, in effect, uncritically accepted something very close to the version of the North Wales story that had originally been disseminated by the *Independent on Sunday*.[19]

The decision not to publish this report was taken at the end of March 1996. One of the main reasons for this decision was that the report contained the names of a large number of people against whom uncorroborated allegations of abuse had been made. The report was therefore effectively unpublishable because of the threat of multiple libel actions. The *Independent on Sunday*, however, was given access to a leaked copy and responded almost immediately with the claim that the truth was being suppressed. 'Paradoxically,' wrote Roger Dobson, the freelance journalist who has been covering the story for some two years, 'the latest attempt to suppress the truth may be what finally brings it the attention it deserves.'

The dramatic full-page article in which this suggestion was made appeared on 7 April 1996. Its publication effectively marked the beginning of one of the fiercest, most persistent and most powerful campaigns run by a national newspaper in the recent history of British journalism. In a matter of days a special logo had been created showing a photograph of a distressed child alongside the heading 'VICTIMS OF THE ABUSERS'. Over the next few weeks both the *Independent on Sunday* and the *Independent* used this device to flag story after story about allegations of child abuse in North Wales and elsewhere.

Throughout the month of April the campaign mounted by the *Independent* seemed to gain momentum with every day. On Monday 22 April the newspaper's coverage of the issue included a front-page story, a three-quarter-page spread on page 2, a first leader entitled 'Rooting out the Abusers', a substantial op-ed article by Allan Levy, QC, entitled 'Our Dereliction of Duty', and a letter from the chairman of the British Association of Social Workers offering 'heartiest congratulations' on the story the paper had run the previous Saturday under the headline 'ABUSERS' CHARTER GOES UNCHECKED'. All these pieces effectively appeared under the banner of the paper's front-page headline, which read: 'PAEDOPHILES "CONTROL CHILDREN'S HOMES"'.

On a number of occasions the newspaper now endorsed the view that a paedophile ring had been operating in North Wales throughout the 1970s and 1980s. On 9 June 1996, exactly two months after it had run its first full-page story about 'the suppression' of the Jillings report, the *Independent on Sunday* dramatically enlarged its original claim about North Wales. Basing its story entirely on the results of the massive trawling operation which was being conducted by the Cheshire Police, the paper now suggested that a *national* paedophile network was at work. Under the bleak two-word headline 'OUR

GULAG' the main story was introduced in large type: 'Victims of organised child abuse in Cheshire homes have at last told all. Their testimonies may unlock national paedophilia networks.' Although the police officer leading the Cheshire investigation has clearly stated that no evidence of organised abuse was uncovered, the way in which the story was presented effectively inverted this view. Its main claim was that events in Cheshire demonstrated that what had allegedly happened in North Wales was not a 'one off'. The paper went on implicitly to endorse the claim made by Clwyd county councillor Malcolm King that children's homes were 'a gulag archipelago' of sexual abuse stretching across Britain.

This story was accompanied by one of the most unusual illustrations which has ever appeared in a quality British newspaper. Printed over the full length of the page was a black silhouette of a leering, large-nosed man with his hands close to the throat of a tearful young boy. Only by reading the text printed alongside was it possible to establish that this was not an attempt to revive the ancient anti-semitic charge of ritual murder, but that the man was supposed to be one of the members of a new evil conspiracy – the national paedophilia network referred to in the story's headline, for whose existence the story itself provided no evidence.

By now the massive press campaign which had been conducted by the *Independent* and the *Independent on Sunday* was beginning to have an impact on many areas of public life. The story was taken up by both radio and television news and by a number of other newspapers, including, at one point, the *Guardian*. Questions were asked in parliament, and Labour opposition spokesmen began to put pressure on their opposite numbers and on the Welsh Office to hold the public inquiry which the *Independent* was now demanding.

On 13 June 1996 a presenter on the BBC radio programme *The World at One* suggested that we might have to face up to the possibility that abuse in children's homes was 'the norm' rather than the exception. By this time, however, the *Independent*'s campaign had already achieved its main objective. At the cabinet meeting which had taken place that morning, as *The Times* would later report, the Prime Minister, John Major, had had to 'read the riot act' to his ministers in order to force them to take action regarding children's homes.

On 17 June 1996 William Hague, Secretary of State for Wales, announced that a full Tribunal of Inquiry would examine the ques-

tion of the alleged abuse of children in care in North Wales. In July
the tribunal was formally appointed by parliament and it was
announced that Sir Ronald Waterhouse, a retired High Court judge in
the family division with local Welsh connections, had agreed to serve
as its chairman.

This tribunal began hearing evidence in January 1997. It is still in
progress as I write and its report is due in the autumn of 1998. One
of the reasons why it would be neither prudent nor responsible to
refrain from public discussion of some of the larger issues involved
until that report appears is that the most dangerous effects of the new
moral panic have not been felt within North Wales and will not be
covered by that report.

This is because one of the immediate consequences of the moral
panic encouraged by a newspaper campaign throughout the spring
of 1996 was to intensify the investigations into care homes which had
already begun in other regions of the country. At the same time police
forces who had not embarked on such investigations were encouraged to launch inquiries of their own.

These were by no means the only ways in which the events that
led to the setting up of the North Wales Tribunal actually deepened
and intensified tragedies unfolding elsewhere. For the massive publicity given to allegations of abuse against care workers throughout
1996 as a result of the *Independent*'s campaign created a climate of
prejudice at a time when a number of care workers who have always
protested their innocence were actually standing trial. Almost all
these care workers were convicted and some of them received exceptionally long sentences.

These effects have been most serious in regions of the country
which fall quite outside the scope of the North Wales Tribunal, and
the evidence which is now accumulating in Cheshire, Merseyside
and elsewhere suggests that they have helped to bring about what is
probably the gravest and most complex series of miscarriages of
justice in modern British history.

*

Although I have concentrated in this short book on retrospective
allegations against care workers which have been collected during
police trawling operations, the problem of false allegations is, it

need scarcely be said, a much broader one.

Partly because of the immense power of sexual evidence and obscene testimony, the whole field of sexual offences has always been especially hazardous. Many ancient religious cultures, including Judaism and Islam, recognise this in their laws on sexual offences such as adultery. The requirement that convictions in such cases cannot be obtained unless there are witnesses is often dismissed by modern commentators as an absurdity. In some respects it is. Yet what this requirement implicitly acknowledges is the frequency of false allegations in such cases and the potentially tragic consequences of treating such allegations as sufficient evidence on which to convict.

The danger of upholding such rigorous evidential standards is that it may become difficult or impossible to gain any convictions at all in sexual cases. It was partly because of the perception that such a state of affairs had come about in the United States during the 1970s that feminist activists sought to accord a new status to the testimony given by children in cases involving allegations of sexual abuse. What made this approach profoundly dangerous was the attempt to buttress moves towards justifiable legal reform with an informal ide-ological obligation to 'believe the children'. When this formula was effectively reapplied to *all* allegations of child sexual abuse, whether made contemporaneously by young children or retrospectively by adults, many of the ingredients of the tragic miscarriages of justice which are now taking place were brought together.* When the pae-

---

* The belief that most of the allegations about sexual abuse in residential care have actu-ally been made by children is widespread. At the height of the campaign which was mounted by the *Independent* in the spring of 1996 I spoke to one of the staff reporters who was dealing with the story and suggested that in relation to some allegations a measure of scepticism might be appropriate. 'Are you saying,' she asked me, 'that we shouldn't believe the children?' Her response suggested that she simply didn't understand that almost all the allegations in question had been made by adults over the age of twenty-five. Residues of the same attitude are sometimes found elsewhere. In a telephone inter-view I conducted with Detective Superintendent Ackerley of the North Wales Police, he explained that during the North Wales investigation he had tried to make sure that 'the children' had a choice about where they could turn to make complaints. When I queried his use of the word 'children' he immediately substituted 'adults' and accepted that he had in fact been referring to thirty-year-old men. Another expression which has some-times been used in discussing these investigations is the curious and significant phrase 'former children'.

Even in cases which really do involve children, taking up the position that we must 'believe the children' is dangerous – for the reasons already discussed. To fail to recog-nise that children are vulnerable to influence and can sometimes make allegations which are *not* true is in itself a form of neglect. Safeguarding vulnerable children from the tragic consequences which can flow from the influence of over-zealous adults is, or ought to be, one of the most fundamental duties of all child protection work.

dophile-ring theory of abuse was applied to care homes at almost the same time that the legal criteria for 'similar fact' evidence were relaxed, the recipe was almost complete.

What made the tragedy far greater than it might otherwise have been was that the new power of accusation which came with the Californian model of child protection, though frequently pioneered by well-intentioned feminists with genuinely subversive ideals, was rapidly learned and usurped by the very men whose authority they had sought to challenge. Directors of social services, senior policemen, psychiatrists and respected barristers were among those who became imbued with the new ethos, and the power which it could confer. Politicians and journalists were, in some cases, equally vulnerable.

As a result, a particular approach to child protection, which had been pioneered in California by radical feminists, rapidly established significant footholds in the social work culture, first of America, and subsequently of many English-speaking countries, including Canada, the United Kingdom, Australia and New Zealand. And having done this, it began to spread further into police forces, the legislature and the judiciary.

Because of its very visibility in the culture of social work, many, though by no means all of the worst excesses of the Californian model have already been countered, and responsible and moderate social workers remain alert to the damage this model can cause. But, largely because our more general culture is still in thrall to a powerful combination of puritanism and sexual prurience, this model of child protection has retained great power: indeed, it appears to have been absorbed almost invisibly into the culture of some police forces and some newspapers and its assumptions have actually become the environment in which some crimes are investigated and some stories reported. Like all environments, this one has tended to become invisible, and because of this invisibility some of its gravest tragedies have yet to be recorded or even noticed.

The idea that our children's homes were taken over during the 1960s and 1970s by an organised network of paedophiles has emerged directly from this environment. This might yet prove to be the most dangerous of all the conspiracy theories which have grown out of the modern culture of child protection. What lends this idea its power is precisely its plausibility and its seeming reasonableness. In terms of cultural history an ancient demonological fantasy – namely that we are surrounded by a conspiracy of evil-doers intent on harming innocent children – has been grafted on to a modern empirical truth. The fantasy that children's homes have been taken over by paedophiles thus draws sustenance and strength from the undeniable fact that sexual abuse does sometimes take place in such homes. Every time a care worker is convicted, the fantasy *seems* to be vindicated. Since it would appear that we have developed a form of investigation which is capable of securing convictions even against care workers who are completely innocent, we have in practice created the conditions where a baseless fantasy seems to be endlessly self-confirming.

What is perhaps even more disturbing is that once the power of fantasy to mobilise the resources of police forces and social workers has been deployed on a small number of occasions, and once a significant number of convictions has been obtained in the investigations which result, the fantasy itself becomes redundant. Future investigations can be justified not by appealing to the spectral evidence of a non-existent paedophile ring, but by a seemingly hard-headed reference to the convictions which have been obtained in earlier investigations.

*

In this essay and throughout this brief book I have tried repeatedly to stress that a significant number of the retrospective allegations of sexual abuse made in relation to care workers are genuine. It is extremely important that this should be clearly and widely recognised. The idea that sexual abuse does take place in care homes is *not* a fantasy and any suggestion to the contrary should be firmly rebutted. But at the same time I have also quite deliberately made the suggestion that a large number of the allegations of sexual and physical abuse collected as a result of police trawling operations and other similar exercises have been fabricated. This is a very grave charge. I have made it for the simple reason that false allegations themselves can, and usually do, have very grave consequences. Having seen at first hand the devastation which can be caused, not only to those who are accused, but to their families, I believe that it is time we recognised both the power and the prevalence of such false allegations.

In the current climate a false allegation of sexual abuse is one of the most dangerous and destructive weapons there is. To make such a weapon readily available to people who are themselves deeply damaged and who sometimes have long records of deception and dishonesty is in itself an act of extraordinary folly. To arrange matters so that we actually make it relatively easy to obtain large financial rewards by fabricating allegations is to compound a folly with a madness. The only reason that we have continued in this state of folly for as long as we have is that most of us do not have to suffer the consequences. And we do not generally encounter those who do. For they are in prison. Unless we awake from our madness quickly and take steps to undo the damage we have already done, they are likely to remain there for a very long time.

Of course it will be objected that those who advance the view that a large number of retrospective allegations of sexual abuse are false are undermining the credibility of the many people who have genuinely been abused while in care. Not only this but they are causing considerable emotional harm by so doing. This is a significant objection and it is extremely important to recognise its force. It is quite true that, in any situation where false allegations are allowed to proliferate, those who have made well-founded accusations may feel distressed and threatened when unfounded ones are exposed. It is precisely for this reason, however, that false allegations should be exposed sooner rather than later. For if they are treated as if they were genuine then the entire currency of complaints becomes debased and there is a grave danger that children who really are being abused (or adults who have been abused in the past) will find themselves once more being systematically disbelieved – as has happened before with tragic results.

It is now clear that during the development of what I have called 'the great children's home panic' a large number of highly improbable allegations have been accepted without question by people in positions of influence and power. These allegations have been believed, it would seem, not because they are inherently plausible but because they are inherently horrific. Unable to accept that large numbers of such horrific and obscene allegations could ever have been made up, people have timidly acceded to their power and held them to be truthful. They have sometimes done so without taking even the most elementary steps to check their veracity. Such credulity has been shown not only by social workers but also by many people whom we are inclined to regard as more hard-headed – journalists and police officers in particular.

Because the members of these professions have played such a significant role in permitting and sometimes promoting the development of the moral panic in which we are now caught up, it is tempting to blame them for what has happened. However, I believe it is extremely important that we should refrain from doing so. In a book which, for all its brevity, contains more serious criticisms of social workers, police officers and journalists than are to be found in some libraries, this plea may seem strangely out of place. But there is an important difference between criticising those who have made serious errors of judgement and *blaming* them for making those errors. Criticism is, or should be, part of an essentially constructive process of analysis. We point out the mistakes which other people have made (or which we have made ourselves) primarily in order to prevent those mistakes from being made again. Blame, however, is almost always part of a destructive process of analysis, and when we seek to pin the blame for complex disasters on individuals or on groups it is very often because we have failed properly to understand what has gone wrong. Quite apart from anything else, blaming other people is an excellent way of avoiding confrontation with our own shortcomings and our own errors of judgement. Perhaps more importantly still, blaming other people, because it blocks the process of proper analysis, makes it very likely that the particular disaster we are inquiring into will happen again.

The police officers, social workers and journalists who have allowed themselves to be caught up in our latest moral panic should certainly bear a considerable responsibility for their own actions. But if we simply blame them for what has happened we are failing to take account of the intolerable pressures we have sometimes placed them under (and these include quite horrific false allegations made, in one case, against an entire police force). We are also failing to take account of the enormous cultural imperatives that have been in play and of the fact that almost all of us have, at one time or another, allowed ourselves to be caught up in the same moral panic. Ultimately it is not the susceptibility of social workers, police officers and journalists to large-scale delusions which we need to examine, but our own.

It is perhaps fitting that these words should be written only a matter of days after news came of the death of one of the scholars who has contributed most to our understanding of the role played by such collective delusions in Judaeo-Christian culture – the French historian Léon Poliakov. Poliakov made it his life's work to study that phenomenon which contains so much of our cultural history, and which speaks so eloquently and so disturbingly about our cultural psychology – anti-semitism. Throughout all the centuries of Christian history there has functioned what Poliakov called 'that terrible mechanism of projection that consists in attributing to the loathed people of God one's own blasphemous desires and unconscious corruption'.[20] The millennial movements of the Middle Ages, the Great European Witch-hunt, modern anti-semitism and Stalin's purges have all been marked by collective fantasies in which groups identifying themselves as the 'pure' have sought to persecute or even annihilate entire groups of human beings imagined as 'evil' or 'unclean'.

We tend to believe that in our civilised late-twentieth-century rationalism and our relative social stability we are no longer vulnerable to such delusions. Yet it is precisely because of our rationalism, and the difficulty we have in acknowledging both our own violence and the full depth and complexity of our sexual imagination, that we are probably more susceptible to dangerous projections than we ever have been. Wherever we allow any group of human beings to be subjected to a process of demonisation, the dangerous fantasies which have been associated with our dreams of purity throughout history will almost inevitably be unleashed. We will begin to imagine the group we have demonised in the same terms which are found at the heart of demonological anti-semitism. They will be seen as members of an evil, highly organised conspiracy intent on infiltrating our national life and harming the very people towards whom our own feelings are most complex and most ambivalent – our children. When small, zealous groups become seized by this kind of fantasy they may well, as happened in the Nottingham satanic abuse case, construct a narrative so powerful that they cannot escape from its grip. There is then a very great danger that they – or the police forces they mobilise – may actually begin unwittingly to 'create' the very evidence they need to empower this fantasy.

Because the fantasy is one to which we are all susceptible it is more than likely that we will fail to recognise what has happened. This danger is particularly acute when, as was the case in demonological anti-semitism itself, a delusion is based upon a palpable reality. For, when fantasy is mixed with fact in unequal proportions, the fantasy can sometimes become even more dangerous and even more destructive.

Over the last ten years one particular group within our own society has been subjected to demonisation: residential care workers. The process by which care workers have been demonised has been complex and has gone through many stages, some of which have already been noted. At the heart of this process is a phenomenon which at first had no specific relationship to residential care. This was the promotion, during the 1980s, of sexual abuse as the greatest imaginable evil. Once the notion of evil had been attached to child sexual abuse a caricature of an imaginary paedophile was gradually created. It was assembled from fragments of fact but the caricature itself was a fantasy. In it we were able to secrete those age-old projections which had traditionally been attributed to the witch, the demonised Jew, or the Devil himself.[21]

Having created a new and believable Devil, our task was to attach to this figure a diabolical conspiracy which was equally credible. With the emergence of the paedophile-ring theory of children's homes this task was gradually accomplished. In the minds of some zealots almost all care workers became paedophiles, or potential paedophiles, or silent abetters of evil crimes which they were presumed to have witnessed or suspected. More moderate observers could see the excesses of this view but at the same time they could not but be affected by it, with the result that almost any care worker was liable to fall under suspicion for the slightest of reasons.

Out of this modern secularised demonology a witch-hunt has developed in which even those who *are* guilty of physically or sexually abusing those in their care have sometimes found themselves facing a bewildering array of false allegations whose seriousness may exceed that of the offences they have in fact committed. Those who are completely innocent have found that their defence has been destroyed during their trial by the sheer weight and number of the false allegations which have been collected against them. When they or their supporters have attempted to protest their innocence they have been met with disbelief, scepticism or indifference. As opposition has been effectively marginalised the new view of care workers has gradually become so powerful and been endorsed by so many eminent authorities, that it seems at times to be almost beyond challenge.

*

Those who read these words in the comfort of their homes may well find that some of the most urgent issues raised are those which concern large questions of cultural psychology and cultural history. But those who read these words, as some will, in the bareness of their prison cells, have other more pressing concerns. If the care workers who are innocent of the crimes of which they have been convicted are to have any hope of success in the appeals which they are preparing, a great deal of work remains to be done.

It will be even more difficult to ensure that their paths on leaving the prison gate do not cross those of other innocent care workers who have just been sentenced. For at the present time it would appear that a third of the police forces in England are engaged in retrospective investigations into care homes and that similar investigations are also in progress both in Wales and in Scotland.

Once again it should be acknowledged that these investigations are likely to result in a significant number of convictions which are either sound or partially sound. But if the pattern of earlier investigations is followed it seems probable that a large number of those convicted will be completely innocent. If we have indeed created a machine for bringing about miscarriages of justice then all the evidence suggests that this machine is gathering momentum almost by the day and that, in the short term at least, it is likely to prove extremely difficult to bring it to a halt.

One of the reasons why, in the midst of our civility and late-twentieth-century scepticism, we have been overtaken by one of the most ancient forms of credulity has been noted already. In our enduring but largely unacknowledged puritanism we remain deeply susceptible to the pornography of righteousness and to the power of obscene testimony. And if we believe that we are not tempted by the power of accusation, then we almost certainly deceive ourselves. It seems likely, indeed, that we will only begin to undo the damage we have caused if we can face up to the heritage of puritanism which we share with the witch-hunters of Salem, and recognise, as Arthur Miller suggested in *The Crucible*, that the impulse to accuse is a part of our nature and that all accusations are, ultimately, a form of confession.

Appendix: The Criminal Injuries Compensation Tariff

THE CRIMINAL INJURIES COMPENSATION SCHEME was set up in 1964. It was originally administered by the Criminal Injuries Compensation Board on a common law basis without there being any standard figures for compensation payments. In 1994, however, a 'tariff of injuries' was published for the first time. This tariff was then withdrawn and replaced towards the end of 1995. A system based on this tariff has been in operation since April 1995. While the Criminal Injuries Compensation Board (CICB) is still in existence and continues to deal with applications for compensation received before 1 April 1996, the new tariff-based scheme is administered by the Criminal Injuries Compensation Authority (CICA), which shares its Glasgow headquarters with the old CICB.

In each year the CICA now expects to receive something in the order of 75,000 applications. Of these only a proportion will be based on allegations of physical or sexual abuse. About 5,000 will contain complaints of *sexual* abuse, of which some 3,000 will relate to alleged incidents outside the family. No specific figure for retrospective allegations of abuse in care homes is available.

The CICA publishes a leaflet in which its compensation scheme is outlined and in which its 'tariff of injuries' is included. The various levels of compensation available range from Level 1 (£1,000) to Level 25 (£250,000). The highest level of compensation is payable only in the case of injuries resulting in very severe disability such as paralysis. The leaflet is freely available on request from the CICA and from most Victim Support Schemes. However, it should be noted that, in residential care cases, many potential complainants are likely to have knowledge of the scheme already, and this was so even before the publication of the tariff in 1995. The section of the leaflet referring to abuse is reproduced below:

Appendix

CRIMINAL INJURIES COMPENSATION SCHEME
TARIFF OF INJURIES

Description of Injury	Levels	Standard amount (£)
PHYSICAL ABUSE OF CHILDREN (WHERE INDIVIDUAL INJURIES DO NOT OTHERWISE QUALIFY)		
Minor abuse – isolated or intermittent assault(s) beyond ordinary chastisement resulting in bruising, weals, hair pulled from scalp, etc.	1	1,000
Serious abuse – intermittent physical assaults resulting in an accumulation of healed wounds, burns or scalds, but with no appreciable disfigurement	5	2,000
Severe abuse – pattern of systematic violence against the child resulting in minor disfigurement	7	3,000
Persistent pattern of severe abuse over a period exceeding 3 years	11	6,000
SEXUAL ABUSE OF CHILDREN (NOT OTHERWISE COVERED BY SEXUAL ASSAULT)		
Minor isolated incidents – non-penetrative indecent acts	1	1,000
Pattern of serious abuse – repetitive, frequent non-penetrative indecent acts	5	2,000
Pattern of severe abuse – repetitive frequent indecent acts involving digital or other non-penile penetration and/or oral genital contact	7	3,000
Pattern of severe abuse over a period exceeding 3 years	11	6,000
Repeated non-consensual vaginal and/or anal intercourse over a period up to 3 years	13	10,000
Repeated non-consensual vaginal and/or anal intercourse over a period exceeding 3 years	16	17,500
SEXUAL ASSAULT (SINGLE INCIDENT – VICTIM ANY AGE)		
Minor indecent assault – non-penetrative indecent physical act over clothing	1	1,000
Serious indecent assault – non-penetrative indecent act under clothing	5	2,000
Severe indecent assault – indecent act involving digital or other non-penile penetration, and/or oral genital contact	7	3,000
Non-consensual vaginal and/or anal intercourse	12	7,500
Non-consensual vaginal and/or anal intercourse by two or more attackers	13	10,000
Non-consensual vaginal and/or anal intercourse with other serious bodily injuries	16	17,500

The standard figures given are for guidance only; multiple allegations can result in multiple compensation payments.

Normally complaints to the CICA must be made promptly, or as soon as is practically possible. But a generous view is normally taken when an allegation refers to the time when the claimant was a child. In the majority of claims which are handled by the CICA a medical examination or a doctor's certificate is a prerequisite for a successful claim. However, in the case of retrospective allegations of sexual abuse there will almost certainly be no medical evidence. In the absence of criminal convictions, the authentication of the alleged crimes will be left almost entirely in the hands of the police. Some reliance may also be placed on reports submitted by psychiatrists or psychologists.

Applications for compensation will almost always be successful if the complaint has resulted in a conviction. A conviction is not necessary, however, in order for compensation to be paid. Both the CICB and the CICA can consider evidence which would not be admissible in a court when deciding whether to award compensation. In a newspaper report which appeared in the *Independent* on 29 April 1996, Ken Badden, an advocate with the CICB, confirmed this: 'The CICB can take account of evidence which the criminal courts are not allowed to admit because we are given wide powers to admit evidence. We have to satisfy ourselves on the bounds of probability. A criminal court has to be satisfied beyond reasonable doubt.' The same article recorded how one claimant had received a four-figure payment even though none of the six people named in his complaints had been prosecuted as a result of his allegations. The case involved retrospective allegations made against care workers.

It is even possible for compensation to be paid when a particular complaint has resulted in a verdict of 'not guilty' in court. This is an entirely logical consequence of the different standards of proof which are applicable. As Ken Badden explained to me, 'The jury are told by the judge, "If you think he did it but you're not sure, you've got to say not guilty." We say, if we think he did it, we pay compensation. And the other thing is that we can take into account evidence that the jury cannot hear. We can be given the opinions of the police officers and the opinions of social workers.'

The views of the police play a very large part in the decision which is reached on any application for compensation. As Ken Badden puts it,

We can receive opinion and evidence which the courts can't so we can say to the police officer, 'What do you think of this, what's the truth?' and if the police officer says, 'Hadn't a shred of doubt about it, but can understand that the jury perhaps weren't sure,' then we can rely on that opinion and attach to it whatever weight we think appropriate. And certainly in North Wales and Cheshire there were a number of cases where maybe the victim was alleging – let's say the victim was alleging ten incidents, maybe only five of them found their way on to the indictment anyway and only three of them led to convictions. If nevertheless we were able to see from all the surrounding evidence and from the opinions of the police officers that all ten incidents occurred then we compensated for the ten incidents, because we were able to say on the balance of probabilities we were satisfied that they all happened.

Although the position described here results in part from the different standards of proof which are applied in criminal and in civil cases, there is another significant factor. This is that the scales are tipped in favour of the complainant by the fact that, because of its constitution, the CICA will not generally concern itself with the case for the defence – at least in the ordinary sense of that word. Except in instances where disputed judgements lead to oral hearings, neither the alleged assailant nor his or her legal representatives will be invited to give evidence. It will often be left to the police to supply both the case for the prosecution and the case for the defence. The grave dangers of relying on the police to authenticate or challenge allegations which they have actually been responsible for collecting does not appear to have been recognised by the CICA.

The CICA may, at its discretion, reduce compensation payments if the claimant has unspent criminal convictions. In order to calculate the reductions which are made in these circumstances, a system of 'penalty points' is operated, with points being awarded according the seriousness of the unspent convictions. Custodial sentences will always be scored highly. However, in 1997 five men who had been judged to have been sexually and physically abused in childhood in care homes run by Liverpool social services won an appeal against the CICB's refusal of compensation because of their later criminal activities. All five were granted awards of up to £20,000 by the authority's chairman, Lord Carlisle, QC. The case was reported by the *Guardian* in the following terms:

The board's decision is likely to have an impact on hundreds of other cases. Lord Carlisle accepted the opinion of a psychologist that the abuse the men had received in the 1970s at children's homes run by Liverpool social services made it difficult for them to form stable relationships in later life – leading to drug and alcohol dependency, anti-social behaviour and crime …

Three of the men, who had been convicted of crimes like burglary, theft and shoplifting in the 1980s, were given full awards of between £7,500 and £20,000. A fourth who had committed several alcohol-related offence and the fifth who had convictions for arson and robbery, were awarded £25,000 and £20,000 respectively, both reduced by 50 per cent. Lord Carlisle said that they had suffered 'appalling abuse' and despite their record they should have at least a reduced award.

Their solicitor, Peter Garsden, welcomed the decision but said he had reservations. 'The board made it clear that it was making a departure from its normal practice and acted leniently. But as the offences all took place after the abuse, I believe that their criminal records should have been ignored.'

The *Guardian* went on to note that Peter Garsden was also bringing a civil action on behalf of 110 men 'who claim to have been abused in four homes in the North-west'. Civil actions of this kind can sometimes result in much higher payments than are made by the CICA and in some sexual abuse cases brought in the civil courts individual complainants have received sums in excess of £100,000.

On 13 January 1998 the *Guardian* reported the case of a thirty-seven-year-old convicted murderer who was suing Leicestershire County Council for £50,000 damages over systematic physical, psychological and sexual abuse he claimed that he suffered when he was taken into care as a child. The man has so far served nearly nineteen years for the buggery and murder of a ten-year-old-boy which he committed in 1978 shortly after coming out of care. He now claims that the crime was one of the consequences of systematic abuse he alleges was inflicted on him by Frank Beck and two other Leicestershire care workers. Leicestershire County Council denied the extent of the abuse he claimed to have suffered. On 8 February 1998, however, the *Mail on Sunday* reported that the man in question had been awarded £50,000 in an out-of-court settlement arranged after an eleven-day hearing in the High Court.

In 1996 the *Independent* published a report in which it was suggested that compensation payments made to men who had alleged abuse while in care might total £40 million. It seems entirely possible that this may turn out to be a conservative estimate.

One phenomenon which is perhaps illuminated by the criminal injuries tariff is the prevalence of allegations of buggery made against care workers. In two cases care workers who were in fact guilty of indecent assaults against boys and who have not contested their conviction in any way, have independently said that that they found themselves facing a significant number of false allegations of buggery – a sexual act which neither of them had ever engaged in. Since they both pleaded guilty to these charges (or some of them) on the advice of their barristers, they would appear to have no motive for misrepresenting the facts now. Although some would argue that they are 'in denial' and are still seeking to minimise the seriousness of their actual behaviour, some of the allegations made against them involved physically improbable or impossible acts. This being so, the more likely explanation is that the care workers in question are telling the truth – and that some of their accusers were not.

It should certainly not be suggested that the CICA is unaware of the problems posed by bogus claims and false allegations. Wherever evidence of bad faith on the part of complainants comes to its attention applications are scrutinised with due scepticism and sometimes rejected. Through no fault of its own, however, it would seem that the CICA has been placed in a situation where evidence of this kind is frequently invisible to it for the simple reason that neither defendants nor their legal representatives are usually allowed to put their case.

Because in practice the CICA is usually compelled to reach a decision after having examined only part of the evidence, and to do so on the basis of paper applications, it would seem to be entirely possible that a significant number of false claims are actually being met. If it is indeed the case that a good proportion of the convictions obtained in retrospective cases against care workers are unsound then it would follow that a *large* number of false claims are being met. The most serious consequence of this is not the drain on the public purse, but the fact that compensation – or the possibility of compensation – would seem to be one of the main lubricants of the machine for creating miscarriages of justice that we have set in motion.

NOTES

1. Strictly speaking these allegations will not be 'uncorroborated' since the doctrine which governs the admissibility of similar fact evidence maintains that the evidence of different complainants is capable of offering mutual corroboration. Some of the dangers attending this doctrine were recognised in 1993 in what may turn out to be a crucial appeal court ruling, *Tinnevely S. Ananthanarayanan* (1993), 98 Criminal Appeal Reports 1 [1994]. This appeal, heard by Lord Justice Steyn, Mr Justice Rougier and Mr Justice Laws, was allowed on the grounds that 'it was ... the judge's task to decide whether there was a real risk that the potentially corroborative evidence was contaminated and if he found such a risk existed he had no discretion to allow the evidence to go to the jury as corroboration.' The case involved a psychiatrist who had been convicted of offences of indecent assault on the evidence of four witnesses. The manner in which evidence was gathered from these witnesses, which led to the view that it might have been contaminated, was strikingly similar to that found in many residential care cases.
2. During a telephone interview which I conducted with Detective Superintendent Ackerley in May 1996.
3. One of the care workers who was acquitted on charges of sexual abuse was also prosecuted separately on several charges of physical abuse, to some of which he pleaded guilty.
4. 'Operation Cleopatra', the investigation into care homes undertaken by the Greater Manchester Police, is reported to have begun after detectives 'received more than forty-eight separate allegations from people now aged in their thirties, forties and fifties'. The newspaper story in which this report was carried, however, went on to make clear that 'much of the impetus for the investigation stemmed from interviews conducted for inquiries into sexual abuse in North Wales, Cheshire and Merseyside'. It would appear that most of the initial allegations were actually collected by neighbouring police forces during earlier trawling operations. It is not clear how many, if any, were made by spontaneously (*The Times*, 20 January 1998).
5. Jean La Fontaine, *Speak of the Devil: Tales of Satanic Abuse in Contemporary England* (Cambridge University Press, 1998), p. 154.
6. Mike McConville, Andrew Sanders and Roger Leng, *The Case for the Prosecution: Police Suspects and the Construction of Criminality* (Routledge, 1991), pp. 87, 79.

7. A revised version of the JET report was prepared for publication in 1990 but was then suppressed. When a version of the report was recently made available on the internet Nottinghamshire County Council attempted to suppress it again by having recourse to an injunction.

8. The authors of the JET report include the following remarks about the Congleton case: 'In the information presented to us at the start of the Enquiry we were informed that in Congleton two separate groups of children who had not had contact with each other talked about babies being killed. They had also talked about people dressed as clowns, people dressed up as animals, lions and tigers and animals being sacrificed. We contacted the investigating police who informed us that the case revolved around three families who were all neighbours. The children concerned belonged to two of the families. The evidence which could be substantiated revolved around sexual abuse only. Whilst the children aged five, six, ten and twelve years were in care they made allegations of attending parties and the murder of a baby named "Daniel" whose body was buried in a back garden. The back garden was excavated and Thermal Image Intensifiers were used. No evidence of a body was found. The allegation was then altered and the body was said to be buried on waste ground. This was also checked and no body was found. The children had made the disclosures during therapeutic work and were believed by the social workers.'

9. The criticisms levelled against Ray Wyre ['Mr W.'] in the JET report have been cited before on a number of occasions. Wyre routinely seeks to fend off these criticisms by arguing that satanic elements were already present in the Nottingham case before his own intervention. If the term 'satanic elements' is construed broadly enough this is undoubtedly correct. But Wyre's argument misses the point. Nobody could reasonably suggest that he single-handedly 'created' a satanic scare. At the root of the problem was clearly a predisposition to believe in allegations of satanic abuse on the part of a number of Nottinghamshire social workers – and on the part of many other people as well. Wyre's own well-intentioned zeal merely exacerbated a problem which already existed.

10. Florence Rush, quoted in Louise Armstrong, *Kiss Daddy Goodnight* (New York: Pocket Books, 1978), p. 133.

11. Florence Rush, 'Freud and the Sexual Abuse of Children', *Chrysalis*, 1, 1977. For a discussion of Freud's significance in the new ideology of child sexual abuse, see my essay on the recovered memory movement, 'Freud's False Memories', which is published as the Afterword to *Why Freud Was Wrong: Sin, Science and Psychoanalysis* (Fontana Press, 1996), pp. 511–28. See also the account of Freud's seduction theory given in the main body of the book, pp. 195–213.

12. Roland Summit, 'The Child Sexual Abuse Accommodation Syndrome', *Child Abuse & Neglect*, 7, 1983, p. 191. Summit's views are discussed by Debbie Nathan and Michael Snedeker in their outstanding study of the satanic scare

in the United States, *Satan's Silence, Ritual Abuse and the Making of a Modern American Witch Hunt* (New York: Basic Books, 1995). The first chapter of this book provides an excellent account of the emergence of what I have called 'the Californian model of child protection'.

13. The most striking research into this kind of confabulation by children is that of Stephen Ceci. See, for example, Stephen J. Ceci and Maggie Bruck, 'Child Witnesses: Translating Research into Policy', Social Policy Report, Society for Research in Child Development, 1993, vol. 7, pp. 1–30.

14. For a brief history of the satanic scare see my article 'A Global-Village Rumour', *New Statesman*, 27 February 1998, pp. 45-6. By far the best accounts of the development of satanic abuse allegations are those which deal with the American origins of the scare. See in particular Nathan and Snedeker, *Satan's Silence*, which brilliantly documents the emergence of what I have called 'the Californian model'. See also Jeffrey S. Victor's excellent *Satanic Panic: The Creation of a Contemporary Legend* (Chicago: Open Court, 1993).

15. The words quoted are those of the journalist Rosie Waterhouse in an article published in the *Independent on Sunday* on 12 August 1990. Waterhouse was one of the first journalists to direct proper scepticism towards the claims made about satanic cults, and the *Independent on Sunday* was one of the few newspapers which did not succumb to a delusion which achieved considerable currency elsewhere in the press. It was this record of proper scepticism which gave the *Independent on Sunday*'s later reports about paedophile rings in children's homes so much authority. These reports, largely researched by freelance journalist Dean Nelson, began to appear in December 1991 when the paper broke the story of Bryn Estyn and North Wales on its front page. They have continued ever since, most recently under the authorship of another freelance journalist, Roger Dobson.

So far as the resilience of the belief in satanic abuse is concerned, it should be noted that one of the main refuges of this belief now is in psychotherapy. See Valerie Sinason, ed., *Treating Survivors of Satanist Abuse* (Routledge, 1994). A number of journalists also retain their belief in satanic abuse. Perhaps the most significant voice in this respect is that of Beatrix Campbell. In 1990 Campbell published a number of articles in the *New Statesman* under such titles as 'Hear No Evil' and 'Satanic Claims Vindicated'. Eight years later she remains a powerful advocate of such views.

16. La Fontaine, *Speak of the Devil*, p. 11.

17. The Nottingham JET report cites an NSPCC statement which recorded in 1990 that 'an increasing number of the society's child protection teams are dealing with children who have been ritualistically abused'. Even earlier than this, on 17 July 1989, the charity had issued a press release stating that it was becoming increasingly 'anxious about the existence of ritualistic abuse involving children'. This press release was picked up by the Press Association and, by the next day, reports based on it had appeared throughout Britain: papers in Aberdeen, Carlisle, Coventry, Edinburgh, Exeter, Kettering, Plymouth,

Wolverhampton, Wrexham and York all carried the story (see La Fontaine, p.165).

The NSPCC was also one of the first organisations to raise concern about sexual abuse in children's homes. On 17 March 1992, following the launch of the NSPCC's annual report, the *Times* carried a story about institutional abuse under the headline 'HUNDREDS ABUSED IN CARE'. Having noted that cases of institutional abuse had come to light in at least eight counties, the director of child care services Jim Harding was quoted as saying 'I don't know how big the iceberg is but I'm sure there are other cases to come to light'. In pursuit of an entirely legitimate and well-founded concern, the NSPCC sometimes engaged in alarmist rhetoric such as this. The NSPCC was closely involved in the North Wales case, having the main responsibility for manning a hotline which helped to collect large numbers of allegations from former residents of care homes.

18. The reasons for what *appears* to be a complete switching of position by these newspapers are complex and fascinating and reveal a great deal about contemporary cultural attitudes. I hope to analyse these reasons elsewhere.

19. The Jillings report, which remains unpublished, did not explicitly endorse the idea that a paedophile ring was operating in North Wales children's homes, but left this open as a possibility.

20. Léon Poliakov, *The History of Anti-Semitism* (Routledge and Kegan Paul, 1974), vol. 1, p. 274. Léon Poliakov died on 8 December 1997. An obituary appeared in the *Guardian* on 12 January 1998. It would be wrong not to mention in this connection the work of Poliakov's most distinguished colleague in this country, the British historian Norman Cohn. Cohn has done more than any other scholar to illuminate the role played in history by collective fantasies. See Norman Cohn, *Europe's Inner Demons: An Enquiry Inspired by the Great Witch-Hunt* (Paladin, 1976); *The Pursuit of the Millennium: Revolutionary Millenarians and Mystical Anarchists of the Middle Ages* (Paladin, 1970); *Warrant for Genocide: the Myth of the Jewish World Conspiracy and the Protocols of the Elders of Zion* (Penguin, 1970).

21. A study of the headlines which have accompanied recent news stories about sexual abuse and paedophiles indicates just how literal the process of demonisation has sometimes been. As can be seen from the front cover of this book, headlines such as 'DEMONS OF THE DARK' and 'DEALING WITH THE DEVIL' are relatively common. Nor has the process of demonisation gone unremarked by other commentators. One of the most perceptive pieces about this process actually appeared in the *Independent* itself soon after its massive children's home campaign had begun to wane. In 'Return of the Angel' Bryan Appleyard noted that 'children today are seen as being at unprecedented risk from a world-wide epidemic of paedophilia. Whole pages of broadsheet newspapers are routinely devoted to today's crop of paedophile horrors … What is clear is that the sexual abuse of children currently enthralls the world … Why have we fastened on to child abuse as the defining evil of our day?

The answer is obvious. Just as a moral, intellectual and cultural vacuum obliges politicians to adopt the child as the only absolute good, so it obliges everybody else to adopt the abuse of the child as the only absolute evil. Look at how social workers became obsessed with Satanic child abuse – dressing up this evil, borrowing the imagery of religion to make it as foul as possible. Child abuse was all they had. There was nothing else on which they could all agree to vent their sense of evil and which they knew would inflame ours. It worked. Perhaps we have dropped the horns and cloaks out of embarrassment. But the sheer intensity of our interest and concern makes the same point – this crime above all others fulfils our need for evil ... Of course children should be cared for and child abusers hunted down and prosecuted. But to become obsessed with these processes indicates that we are not confident we can do either, that there is something so wrong with the present that we must flee to the future we imagine to be embodied in our children. They will not thank us because children, unlike their parents, still believe in growing up.' (*Independent*, 29 August 1996).

On a different but related matter it seems important, given the significance I have attached in this essay to the process of projection, to point out that 'projection' is not, in its origins, a psychoanalytic concept. The process of projection was described much more perceptively by some pre-Freudian writers than it was by Freud himself. I discuss this issue in the preface to the paperback edition of *Why Freud Was Wrong*, p. xiii–xiv. See also the discussion of psychoanalysis itself as a form of demonological projection, pp. 326–9.

A BRIEF HISTORY OF BLASPHEMY
LIBERALISM, CENSORSHIP AND 'THE SATANIC VERSES'

Richard Webster

In this study of the Rushdie affair Richard Webster surveys the history of blasphemy and goes on to examine in detail the conflict which arose over *The Satanic Verses*. What he sees is not a battle between authoritarianism and freedom but a clash between two forms of rigidity, two kinds of fundamentalism.

'Remarkable, bold and vigorously written...worthy of the age of Burke indeed...grave and sensible.' BERNARD CRICK, *Political Quarterly*

'Treads an exceptionally fair-minded and intellectually rigorous path between the orthodoxies and illiberalisms on both sides.' RICHARD HOGGART

'I was immensely impressed by it, and by its resistance to cant, and above all by its humanity and essential tolerance.' JOHN LE CARRÉ

'Instructive, elegantly argued and *full* of startling and important ideas.' RANA KABBANI

'Although Webster insists he is not a disciple of Orwell, or anyone else for that matter, he shares Orwell's readiness to contest the received ideas of the intellectual establishment.' RICHARD WEST, *The Times*

THE ORWELL PRESS
A Paperback Original

WHY FREUD WAS WRONG
SIN, SCIENCE AND PSYCHOANALYSIS

Richard Webster

'Freud, as revealed in *Why Freud Was Wrong*, is no independent and fearless thinker, but a man who repeatedly fell under the spell of charismatic healers, and who behaved like the messianic founder of a great faith rather than the discoverer of a scientific truth... Webster's systematic analysis of Freud is of a man driven by ambition... Precisely because he is at pains to give Freud the benefit of the doubt at virtually every turn, he is arguably the most devastating critic of them all.' ANTHONY CLARE, *The Sunday Times*

'Masterly... covers a lot of intellectual ground with great clarity and verve.' JEROME BURNE, *The Independent*

'*Why Freud Was Wrong* is a delight to read: it is informative and humane but also powerful, pugnacious and controversial. You will not quite be the same when you put it down as when you started.' ANDREW SIMS, *The Tablet*

'The greatness of Webster's book lies not only in its command of the primary and secondary literature, nor only in its wonderfully lucid and witty prose, but in the penetration of his understanding of the man and his influence.' RAYMOND TALLIS, *The Lancet*

A FONTANA PRESS PAPERBACK